G000077674

GLASGO'

by

Robbie Moffat

PALM TREE PUBLISHING

PALM TREE PUBLISHING
Paisley, Scotland Pa1 1TJ

First published in paperback JANUARY 2109

Typeset: Verdana 10pt

ISBN-10: 0 907282725
ISBN-13: 9780907282723

INTRODUCTION

In movies the image is still very much controlled. The actors are put in their best clothes - or at least clothes that have been selected to reveal something about their character - it is a sham. Likewise the photography of the 50's and 60's. They are portraits - often self portraits as the person in front of the camera has asked the person behind the camera to take the photograph for them. It is a moment in time that they wish to capture - they are saying - this is me and I am happy with the way I want to be remembered. Its a fix.

I have a problem with this and I think it shows when I am being photographed. I would like to be captured in that moment of time but I do not know how to sum up that moment for the photographer. This makes me a difficult subject to photograph. This is quite something when you consider that I have been the cinematographer (the guy operating the camera) on sixteen of my own movies. Maybe that's why I stay behind the camera - to avoid making real images of myself .

I certainly feel more adept at creating a self-portrait in words than in images. It makes the portrait less ambiguous. A picture may speak a thousand words but these words will change with the viewer. No, I think what I am trying to say - that as I search for the truth about who I am and what I have become in time, I discover that the truth is a hazy landscape covered in a blanket of mist.

So why I would write down some of the things that happened to me in my early life is easily explained - I want to have a look at what I've done and at the end of the process be able to say 'I never followed the monkey path'.

At the point of starting this book I had no agent, no publisher and not even an inkling of an audience. Unlike actors or performers I have never been in front of the camera. However, I had been encouraged by those around me to spill the beans, pop the toast, and serve up something edible.

So now we are going to find out.

The funny thing is - when someone asks you if you have met anyone famous my first reaction is no. When you meet someone famous - firstly you are star struck or at least slightly in awe, then after awhile they become human, exhibit the same flaws, sometimes even more acutely so than someone in your own family or a friend might reveal. Most times you like them, then boy oh boy, sometimes you don't.

But this book is primarily about me before I became and adult and knew what I wanted to do with my life, who I am, what I am about, how I've got to the place I wanted to go (partly), how I exceeded my own expectations, and finally the realisation that I still have a long way to go.

My thanks to everyone who has put up with me from the moment I was born until the present day. I wouldn't be the person I am without a single one of you.

Robbie Moffat

GEOGRAPHY AND HISTORY

I made my first feature film in Glasgow. This was not an accident; it probably was a consequence of having been born there.

The adage in the writing business is that you write what you know and I think that by in large I agree with that. There are exceptions - I have not lived in the sixth century, I have not experienced abandonment on an island for thirty years, I have not been on a space ship hurtling towards the edge of the universe - like I said, there are exceptions. But when it comes to getting started in any kind of writing art form - poetry, novels, plays, screenplays - I always started with what I knew- I drew mainly from my own life experience.

I was born in Stobhill Hospital, Springburn, Glasgow at 10.35am on the 25th March 1954. I was nine pounds thirteen ounces and the doctor declared to my mother that I was longest baby he had ever delivered. I was measured and pronounced to be twenty-four inches long - that's sixty centimeters, so I must have been curled up like a snake in my mother, as she was only five foot two inches tall.

Whether this is an accurate account of my first appearance in the world or not, the story came from my mother herself when I was very young, so why should I question it, she was there! Sometimes fact is stranger than fiction and perhaps there is some truth to it as I grew to be six foot three inches by the time I was fifteen.

My mother Isabella Moffat was a domestic servant. My father was registered as unknown, and to this day I do not know who my father is/was. As a child I was not particularly interested in finding out as it was obvious that whoever it was had caused my mother a lot of pain. More than that I think, she was ashamed. Not of me, but the fact that she could not speak about him to me or any of the rest of her family which was an enormous family by today's standards.

My grandfather George was one of sixteen children, and my mother one of a mere six. My grandmother Mary Brown Ramsay was the daughter of a Linlithgow milliner but instead of moving up to the middle-classes, my grandfather then a miner in Rosewell, managed to descend her and his family including my mother into tenement poverty in West Russell Street, Cowcaddens, a notorious rough part of Glasgow (street now gone).

As a child I did not see any of the poverty, I did not know anything else and my first residence may have been in that one room and kitchen gas-lit tenement in Callander Street that my grandparents inhabited from the Second World War onwards, now a car park. **

My birth certificate gives my mother's usual residence as 50 Craigendmuir Street which is in Provanmill, East Glasgow, and that, if I remember right, was where my Auntie Mary and Uncle Richard lived with my cousins the Hobans. The Hobans are a whole different story but I am grateful to my cousins Brian, George and Ian for their gang connections and teaching me how to take on bullies and win.

So my first two years are a blur. I don't really remember where I lived except that I remember staying at Auntie Robina's (my mother's eldest sister), Auntie Margaret's (my mother's first cousin), as well as Auntie Mary's and my grandparents. I was farmed out to pre-nursery at the age of four months as my mother had to work.

I never knew where that nursery was until forty years later. All through the Nineties I had a puppet company and I performed anywhere and everywhere in Central Scotland for ten years. Towards the end of this period I was asked to perform in a small children's pre-nursery in the east end of Glasgow. The moment I walked into the place I knew it. It was a very old building and suddenly the memories of being a baby came flooding back to me.

I did my show and as I was leaving there were two small rooms along a small corridor. The doors were open and as I looked into one of the rooms I saw a child's cot with the high sides of the type that I had been so often placed in. Being born two feet long and being bigger than the other babies my age made me a handful. Being placed in one of these cots by the nurses had been their way of breaking some of my wilfulness.

Naturally it did not work, but this was the room where I was isolated and left to cry all my early tears. I felt unwanted. My mother loved me with all her heart and worked to provide for me, but it left me with an emotionally detached nature for decades. I did not understand it immediately, but when I transferred to nursery school proper at the age of two and a half, I knew I was on my own, that the world was not fair, and that somehow I had been singled out as the difficult kid.

To top it all, I was left-handed. Hence my hatred of porridge. There are not many Scotsman who will admit to that. The wilfulness that had got me into so much trouble at pre-nursery continued at nursery proper as they tried to make me bend to the system. In the cot detention phase I learned that if I threw my golliwog out of the cot and bawled long enough, I would get my golliwog back. All I really wanted was someone to say 'Aw what a lovely wee boy you are' rather than treating me like the little bastard child I was growing up to be.

For some reason Glaswegians back then did not give their children teddy bears - so I got a home knitted golly. I loved my golliwog - he was my best pal but he looked nothing like me or anything else I had ever seen in my life. To this day I still do not know whose idea it was to give me a golliwog. When I first got him I treated him rotten - remember he was in detention with me and it was him I took it out on. I do not know what happened to my golly but by nursery school I no longer needed him, I was going to handle adults on my own.

In many ways my time at nursery school can be viewed as a tragedy and a triumph. They succeeded at making me right handed, I succeeded in working my way through being locked in cupboards, breast smothered, fighting, and the challenges of language to come out the other end as wilful as ever. In the end I gave into the right handed thing for two reasons - firstly, to stop the force feeding of me with porridge every morning with a spoon in my right hand - and secondly, because it made me ambidextrous and I started to see some advantage in that. When I got into fights I was now using both fists.

The first fight I remember was my cousin Hughie Barrie. I was two and a quarter and he was two months older than me. He had a tricycle (it must have been tiny) and we got into a fight over who should be riding it. In fairness, it was his bike, but he was my cousin so we were family - what was his was mine and vice versa. When we came to blows a thought flashed through my mind that is as vivid to me today as it was then. If I don't beat him I will be bullied the rest of my life.

That single thought went on to shape my entire childhood. Glasgow was and still is one of the most violent environments in the United Kingdom to be raised in. If you do not learn to fight, then you have to find someone who will fight for you. In the end if you learn to fight, then you become the one who also fights for those who cannot fight for themselves. In a sense you overcome bullying within your own age group but you are then called upon to protect your pears from the bullying of bigger and older boys. The moment I made Hughie cry and won the fight, I set a course that would last until I was sixteen - that's fourteen years of constant expectation and preparation to be in a fight at anytime with anybody.

That is the Glasgow of my childhood.

Recently I was asked if I thought that Glasgow had changed. How do I know? I'm not a kid in Glasgow these days. However, instinct tells me that the answer is no, it has not changed. It may have changed for the visitor, but it is a change of perception not culture. Whether it is liked or not, the West Coast Scottish male is a product of centuries of fierce independence and a willingness to fight for principle not for the love of it.

Every fight I had, I wished I had not had to do it, but I did because most times I had to because something was at stake. In nearly all occasions it was the belief that what I was doing was right - I was fighting to preserve a safe environment in which to play and in which to allow education to flourish for myself, and those I fought on behalf of.

In all those years I only lost one fight at the age of twelve. I have a broken bone in my nose as a keepsake. I wish I had avoided that one but I could not. We had a lot of boys at my primary school from the Boy's Home in Eastwood, at one stage one third of the entire intake of a school with a hundred and twenty boys and girls of all ages. As individuals I had sympathy for them - they were from broken homes, orphans, neglected.

But on another level they were scarily organized, with steal-toe capped shoes and no parents to haul in front of the headmaster. After almost five years of keeping the peace and keeping these kids feeling wanted during their usually short stay at the school, a lad called Glass-Eye Jim Gillespie joined our midst. Ginger haired, sturdy, mouthy and as big as me with enormous steel-toe caps it was an inevitable showdown.

We had quite a crowd the day of the fight. All around us they had torn down the old tenement buildings and put up spanking new fifteen-storey skyscrapers. Midst the rubble and the new we fought and for the first time in my life I felt real pain. It was a lesson for me. If you fight all of your life you will eventually meet someone bigger who will beat you.

The silver lining was after that fight in which I got a bloody nose and he got a black eye on his good eye, harmony reigned. Gillespie's disruption stopped, and his dad came for him a short time after and took him away to live with him.

When I think back on all that fighting it is the one thing I wish my childhood had gone without. In academic terms I felt fortunate from the age of five to attend Sir John Maxwell Primary in Pollokshaws, the state school closest to where I now lived with my mother and my new step-dad John. The school had been a continuation of the first parish school in 1689, and the first free school for workers children set up in Scotland in 1759 that ironically was now the Boys Home just down the road.

I love Pollokshaws to this day - it is a unique place with a gloriously rich past. Its produced philanthropists and socialist politicians. John MacLean the architect of Red Clydeside communism is a notable worthy. Its present crop of worthies included TV's Taggart Alex Norton and comedian Frankie Boyle. And me of course. But best of all, it is adjacent to the Pollok Estate, now Pollok Park, once owned by the

Maxwell family and donated to the city in 1965.

Back when I was at the primary school, Lady Maxwell came to the prize giving at the Burgh Hall next to the school. Irritatingly to many, as well as being the biggest in my year, I was also fortunate enough to be one of the brightest, but I had to wait until Leonard Goobler and Barbara Cummings, my first girlfriend, left the school when I was nine, before I started to climb those wooden steps onto the stage at prize giving every June.

I did not always have it my own way, for the next three years I had to alternate and second-fiddle with Roddy Mackay at prize time. He could always beat me by one point in two hundred and fifty when he put his mind to it, and I could always just outrun him when I put my mind to it. However, we were both out in front when it came to the rest of our class of thirty-six and that probably made us insufferable. We were popular with the girls but being the 'cool dudes' we kept them at an arm's length.

Like any self-respecting bloke, I've always liked girls. There were loads of them at nursery school including Muriel MacDonald and Linda MacMillan and some of those same girls cropped up in my teenage years though I didn't handle them as well as I should have.

Most of the primary school girls did not

make it to Shawlands Academy secondary. This was because I was in the last year of streaming. Only the top six went from my primary to Shawlands about a mile away. The other thirty went to Hillpark Junior Secondary, the new school perched on Manse Hill overlooking the newly rebuilt Pollokshaws of multi-storey flats and council housing. Roddy, Tommy and Archie the twins, Christine Aitken, June McFeeters, and me. The rest were chucked on the academic scrap heap so to speak.

Injustice? Yes. It was my first inclining that life was a fix. I was angry when I got to Shawlands Academy and discovered that the top thirty at Shawlands Primary School were placed at the Academy and the bottom six at Hillpark. It was my first experience of social injustice on such a large scale. It had nothing to do with merit, it was all about where you lived, and you can imagine my further indignation when I found out they had all had two years of French at the other primaries and it was compulsory at the Academy.

I go to the Cannes Film Festival for ten days every year, and my French is still not good. Was it the fault of my primary teachers? No, it was not. Sir John Maxwell until recent years was the centre for Gaelic learning in Scotland. I was given the opportunity at the age of ten to take Gaelic classes on Saturday mornings and I wanted to but could not. I played for the primary school football team and it clashed.

So no Gaelic for me.

A similar thing occurred at secondary school a few years later. I was in the school chess team as well as football team. In my third year we started playing Wednesday league games and it clashed with the chess training and tournaments. What do you do? I weighed it up. I'm young, I'm fit, and I'll be able to play chess until I'm eighty. Obvious choice in the end, but it was a hard one.

I loved chess. Chess taught me to respect women, really respect them for their minds. When you are in a school junior chess tournament, aged thirteen, and you are playing on board one, and the girl opposite you is from an even poorer background (and that's saying something), and she's a different religion, and you have nothing in common, yet she is still really pretty, you are not prepared for her beating you, and you do not contemplate defeat. But she beat me, and it was a great match. The rest of the team (five others) could not understand how a girl could beat me, but I did. I never underestimated a girl again.

I think my respect for woman shows in my films. Time and time again I seem to make movies that have strong central female figures. In this respect I think I am truer to life than some other film-makers - a son is subservient to his mother, hence we have a matriarchal society, the mother is the dominant force in the culture.

You see this in all Celtic countries, Latin societies, and in India - these are the lands of the mother goddess figure. The land is referred to as she -- the motherland. Germany is the obvious antipathy of this, and I think England is somewhere between both and hovers in a very undecided way depending on which part of the country you come from.

In my case - Celtic background, fatherless early years, dominance of aunts and female first cousins in my informative years - and the influence of my mother, an incredibly strong willed woman - has formed my view of women as easily the equal of men, even superior to them when using all their given faculties.

Of course being a storyteller, I am only dealing in make belief and occasionally I do feel the need to vent a male perspective on life in films like Rain Dogs and Winter Warrior. Yet I cannot help returning to the female psyche, I am fascinated by the endless permutations of female behaviour as killer, lover or careerist.

But I'm getting ahead of myself. My first sense of geography was from the age of two. At the time of my first fight with Hughie, I remember living in Pollok, a large sprawling housing scheme in southwest Glasgow. This is the same area that political activist and city councillor Tommy Sheridan organised his anti-poll tax campaign from in 1990, a fight that he believed enough in to spend six months for in Edinburgh's Saughton Prison.

The area is a strange mix of poverty and politics. During Tommy's fund raising to fight the poll tax I saw the buckets going round filling up with pound coins and spare change but also witnessed at the same time a single mother of three living in a cramped two bedroom slum with peeling wallpaper, damp, no bed of her own, and unable to cope.

Had that been my own childhood? I hope not. If it was I don't remember it as that except that we were left to our own devices a lot usually under the supervision of an older cousin. And there were plenty of them - Marjorie, Isobel, Margaret, Pat, Marilyn, two Johns, Alec, Brian, George, Ian.

As I said, my mother's family was huge by today's standards. I never had any conflict with them - I was happy to have them look after me - and I was their favourite cousin who did not have a father. Part of that favouritism was due to my mother being the family's favourite aunt. She was the youngest and I was born when she was twenty-six. This made me one of the last cousins except for Robina and Grace.

In fact, I am just a day older than Robina and we were thrown together from birth as the cousin twins. I have not seen Robina for a couple of years now - she rose to the dizzy ranks of chief social worker for North Glasgow - but I know when I do see her again at a wedding or funeral it will engage in the same competitive banter and behaviour that started in earnest when she hit me over the head with a saucepan when I was two.

I did not finally get my own back on her until we were thirteen when I picked her up, turned her upside down and then accidentally dropped her on an old tree stump. She has never really forgiven me for that and will surely mention it the next time I see her. I think I have finally forgiven her for hitting me over the head with the saucepan but I am not sure.

Dropping Robina on her head was the last time I treated her as one of the boys. I really did start to see her as a girl, particularly because of her friend Helen Tennant who taught me how to kiss at Robina's thirteenth birthday party at her mum's house in Milton.

Supervised by cousin Isobel who was in the kitchen most of the time making out with Alistair her soon to be fireman husband, I got into an argument with Robina, the only cousin I ever argued with, over the card game we were playing for pennies.

This was a serious argument over the difference between the rules and cheating and it put me off gambling for life. Serious though, I realised that if I could get into a fight over pennies with my 'twin', what would it be like if it was over pounds? Since that day, I have never gambled for money, other things yes, my life, my career, my relationships, but never money.

After Isobel was forced to intervene and Alistair with his good looks smoothed everything over, we had the cake come in, Beanie blew the candles out, we had our cake and ate it. Then on to the kissing lessons that must have gone on for a good forty five minutes.

That Helen was a good-looking girl with dark fringed hair and cheeky eyes. I went on a date with her some months later but we did not really have much in common - I played football, she played netball - I played chess, she played cards - I loved school, she could not wait to leave. This was the story of my life with girls in my early days. Our goals were never the same, our pursuits never overlapped.

On top of that I had no spare time - I did homework classes on Monday, band practice or cross country on Tuesdays, football training on Wednesdays, first aid or signalling or wayfaring Thursdays, Boys' Brigade on Fridays, football games morning and afternoon Saturdays, church and bible class Sundays. I was Solomon Grundy born again on Monday. From the age of eight until I was almost sixteen I never stopped - I had no free time to fit in girls except in the summer holidays.

Perhaps that is why in later years my most successful relationships have been with women who have shared the same professional interests - art, drama and film. However, at the age of two was only able to recognise my surroundings, where it was safe to play, that sort of thing.

I did get my head stuck in the railings on the bridge over the Levern at Levernside Crescent. Genuinely stuck, so much so that one of my cousins got a fireman from the station across the street on Brockburn Road to free me. At the time I must have been three. I was embarrassed but everyone was lovely about it and we all went home for tea.

At that age I was prone to illness - I caught everything under the sun that was contagious - I also got a few other things that weren't so run of the mill. I had whooping cough at four months and I was hospitalised for weeks.

Two years later I developed mastoiditis, a condition caused when bacteria in an eardrum infection extends and inflames the middle ear into the mastoid air cells. Left untreated it becomes life-threatening meningitis, an infection of the outside of the brain, or a brain abscess, a pocket of pus and infection that develops in the brain.

I was hospitalised.

I received antibiotics through an intravenous catheter, and underwent a surgical procedure that involved making a small opening in my eardrum to drain the fluid and relieve the pressure from the middle ear. My hearing was fully restored after the fluid was drained. However, I had ear problems for years, I always had to have earplugs when swimming and told not to put my head under water.

I was twenty five, snorkelling on the Cay coral reefs of Belize with a face mask, before I could overcome this disadvantage, and thus be able to dive down and swim with the barracuda.

At four I had another hospitalisation. My mother took me to see Doctor Robertson, our local GP in Pollok, as I was poorly and complained of having a very sore ear. My ear was just mildly infected, but Doctor R thought that my right knee looked funny. I had got so use to the rumble and tumble of been an active four year old in short trousers that I thought nothing of having skinned knees.

I was hospitalised.

My leg was poisoned and even I could see that it looked swollen compared with my left leg. I was operated on the next day - three holes bored in my leg - two below the knee and one above. When I came round my mother told me that they had saved my leg and had it gone a few more days I would have developed septicaemia.

Lying in bed with my leg up in a sling I marvelled to think that my ears that had taken me to the doctor yet it was my leg that was up in the air. I have now found out that septicaemia can be a direct result of bone infection, or from meningitis, and that kind of links the whole episode back to my ear infection. So it is easy to believe that it had nothing to do with my knees but I don't thing so.

Until I got into long trousers at twelve, my knees gave me regular problems. The knees themselves worked fine, but the sores on them were a constant bane. My mother would make a poultice and bandage my knee overnight to reduce the swelling in the boils. Year on year I rebuilt the skin on my knees just to have it all scraped off again when I started playing competitive football at the age of nine.

I don't think I ever complained. It was about this time of my knee operation that my step-dad John came into my life. I remember vividly a hot sunny day in the summer of 1958 in Carnwardric Road where I was living with my mum when John said he would give me sixpence if I could go the whole day without skinning a knee. I took the challenge.

I was out to play from ten o'clock until four o'clock with 'dinner' (lunch) in between. All day long I managed to avoid getting a scratch - I was really proud of myself and also very amiable with the other kids as I did not want to take part in any rough and tumble in the gutter, or across the street in Carnwardic park. Then about ten minutes before going in, I fell over while running for a ball. I skint my knee. I was completely disappointed in myself - I had lost my bet with my new dad.

I trailed up the short set of steps to the door of the one bed and kitchen cottage flat we were now living in, and John was standing there smiling. He was only twenty-four, blonde haired with glasses like Glenn Miller. He was a handsome man and I was happy my mum had found someone who really loved her.

But I was disappointed I had not equipped myself properly like the smart kid I really was and instead come home with a bleeding knee. John laughed and said he knew I could not do it.

I said I was sorry - I would try harder tomorrow. He said that I was a brave little boy and that I had gone almost the whole day without a scratch and that I deserved the sixpence as I had stuck to my word and tried to do as I was told. He put his hand in his pocket and pulled out a silver sixpence and gave me it to me . With a big smile and a pat on my back, he told me to go into my mum to get my knee washed and a plaster put on it.

And that is how I remember Dad coming into my life. I consider John Aitken my father as he is only father I have known. From the moment he came into my life, my life changed for the better and in a way that could not have been imagined. He was recently returned from his two years national service and had been stationed in Hong Kong. He had returned to Glasgow and finished his training as a plumber and worked for the City Corporation.

As a tradesman he made a decent living, enough to support my mum, and me though mum had been to learn cookery and continued to work as a kitchen assistant and cleaner. She had been working at Pollokshaws Burgh Hall on the night that they had a dance in which my dad attended. It was the rock and roll years of Elvis, Buddy Holly and Bill Hayley. My mum swore that he chased her around and around a table in the kitchen until she agreed to out with him.

My mum was a good cook. She told me she went to cookery school and I believed her. She was an expert.

There was one cookery school in Glasgow, the Glasgow and West of Scotland College of Domestic Science. It had been founded to educated young working class women in culinary skills as a contribution to the improvement of family life among lower income groups. Later, the school became responsible for the training of teachers, the subjects taught initially included superior cookery, plain cookery and cookery for the working classes although in time the syllabus expanded to include diplomas in cookery, laundry, housewifery, dressmaking, needlework and millinery. The School not only taught teacher's diplomas but also provided demonstrations and lectures for the public.

Was this my mum's school? I just do not know, but I do know she was skilled in superior cookery when she needed to be. Generally though, I was fed plain cookery - corn flakes for breakfast (not porridge!), soup and pudding for lunch, mince and potatoes, meat and two veg, pie and mash, stew, fish and chips. As I grew up the food did become more exotic - more varied vegetables, curry, noodles, spag boll, chops - but it was still of a working class nature.

My dad always liked brown bread but it took my mum decades to ditch white bread because it made for easier sandwich making and the crust could be cut off when it had to look fancy. It was an omnivore kind of diet and it suited me just fine - I liked my mum's food.

This fits in with my blood type that is B-.

According to one dietician, B blood folk evolved about 10,000 years ago and survived on a diet of cultivated cereals and vegetables as well as meat. Two percent of the world's population is B-. Is that a good thing? Sounds as though we are a dying breed! B- is the most prominently found in central Asia, particularly India. There are some scientists who believe that our race differences should be classified by blood type rather than skin colour.

I think there is some merit in the idea that race is a culturally engendered notion rather than a scientifically proven fact.

My Mum married John. I remember her preparing for it with cousin Marjory who was only ten years younger than my mum. After they went, my granny watched me. I knew something was going on, as my mum was being really huggy with me in her wedding outfit. I wanted to go to the wedding with her but everyone told me that it would not be sensible.

I understood what they meant. It was 1959 and I was a bastard child. I really did understand it all but I still felt that I should have still been allowed to go and I made a fuss. Nowadays, kids attend weddings whether the parents are married or not, and brides have children by their sides during the ceremony.

Not back in 1959. My parents were married in the parish Church of Scotland in Pollokshaws, the church across narrow Maida Street from the primary school that was to shape my life from the moment they married until I was sixteen.

I got to see the photographs a week later and I thought my mum looked really lovely. Dad looked smart too but it was my mum who stole the pictures - she looked happier than any time I'd ever seen her in public. In private I knew that smile, but at last she was showing it to the world and not just me.

I still think I was the love of my mum's life. When she looked at me with my blonde hair and hazel eyes, I am sure she saw in me the man who had helped to make me. I could just tell that she had loved him and that he had broken her heart. She could never speak to me about it because of the pain it would have caused her.

In return I did not want her to talk about it as I was frightened it would break what we had together - an understanding, a love that needed no words. She would have broken down, and I could not bear that, I too would have been destroyed, and the pair of us would have been no use to anyone for the rest of our lives.

And so the secret was kept to her deathbed.

She died while I was at the Cannes Film Festival in 2005. It was the last day; I was flying back to Glasgow the following afternoon with the intention of seeing her. My sister called at six thirty in the morning. I was still out on the town and I bumped into my LA lawyer friend Rick Rosen and he was the first to hear of my mother's death.

I am not saying that my mother died deliberately before I got back, but deep down I knew that it was her way of letting the secret die with her rather than seeing me for the last time and us finally breaking the silence we had maintained for fifty one years.

I gave the family speech at the crematorium and tried to sum up my mother's achievements in part poem, part prose. I knew the inner heart of my mother as I received the love that came out of it more than anyone else in my early years with her.

As I grew up, she shared much of that love with others, spread it around to my cousins, their children, my sister and brother to come, John, and a host of orphans and strays that came into contact with her.

She was a remarkable woman and I miss her.

After the marriage, life got a whole lot better. We moved to 59 Harriet Street in Pollokshaws, a short tenement street that still had some seventeenth century cottages at the bottom of it by the Auldhouse Burn. The Gorman's lived in one of them and so did the MacGregors. There were about eleven of them in that family.

At the other end of the street was the Round Toll house that housed the Craig's. There were four children, and Pamela was in my class all the way through primary. The Tollhouse is now in the middle of a road island where Pollokshaws Road meets Barrhead Road. Back then it was the Craig's, a tiny little house. I did not know how they all managed to live in such a small dwelling.

I liked Pamela; she was a nice gentle natured girl. Her little brother Tommy always seemed to be snotty nosed and dirty kneed but he always seemed to want to be in our gang though he was far too young.

Our gang ringleaders were Christopher Smith and Eric MacIntosh. Specky Smith was a bully but Tosh knew how to handle him. Tosh was someone to look up to. He could play keepy-up with a ball like nobody else; he taught us how to play cricket in Greenbank Park; and how to play pitch and put in the tenement back yard.

The back yard was grass-less except for the bottom end towards number 67. The yard was hemmed in the east by 1 Greenbank Street, the north by 59 to 71 Harriet Street, the west by the Auldhouse Burn. The south sandstone wall backed on to the park, a small grass field with a cherry tree lined pathway that went right round it.

The yard by comparison was anything but

green - the kids had dug it up long before I ever moved there. From kick-the can to golf, it had been scuffed, gouged and mutilated by us all. The middens in the middle didn't keep it smelling fresh either. In retrospect, it was the back yard of a slum - as near as anything in Peter Mullan's *Fridge* or Lynn Ramsay's *Ratcatcher*.

It might not have been an ideal world, but it was our world, and we were safe playing hide and seek, dreeping the wall, swinging on something. As I grew in that backyard, I eventually escaped regularly into the park until I only played in the park.

This brought a different kind of adventure - making berry-firing crossbows in the autumn to collecting bees in jam-jars in the summer. Why we collected bees I do not know? No one seemed to discourage it or even consider it dangerous. To us it was not, it certainly taught me respect for bees and not to be scared of them.

The dangerous part became the time I was up on the disused garage roof on the other side of the park gate with Neil Houston and we were told to get down by two policemen. I was eight and it was my first brush with the law. The policemen thought we were up to no good and I felt really embarrassed.

Neil was never a lad very good with words so I spoke up. We were collecting bees.
"Bees?" "Its something we do. We keep

them in the jar with some flower heads and we watch them." "Up on the roof of the garage?" "The elderberry flowers attract them" I went on.

One of the policemen looked at me with puzzlement. "You were risking your necks up there to collect bees?" "Yes, the elderberry flowers are right at the top. The only way to get to them was to climb up on to the roof."

The 'polis' shook his head. "I guess we got carried away" I said. They both relaxed a little. Neil and I were just kids.

They warned us that the roof of the garage was unsafe and we could have fallen through. I knew the roof was safe, but I also knew they were right; we both apologized and said we would not do it again. They asked us to let our bees go and then let us run along.

I never collected bees again. I've only ever been stung once and that was an accident between the bee and me. Sometimes I collected wasps and let them go, but my dad had a thing about wasps in the house - he battered them with rolled up newspaper.

I never liked that - I preferred to coax them out the window if I could and today I still do. I currently have a wasp nest on the outside wall of my kitchen and even in winter one sometimes strays in.

There are many echoes of my childhood still in my day-to-day behaviour. I still more or less do the same basic exercises I learned in the Life Boys from the age eight. I still shower or bathe rather than bath.

My mum had always washed me in the sink in our various earlier bathless dwellings and Harriet Street was no exception. It was one story up and the kitchen sink window faced on to the street down which trams, and later buses, would stop at the halt below.

One evening I was being bathed naked in the sink. I looked out and saw the whole top row of the tram staring at me. They had huge amused smiles on their faces. I was mortified!

Quick witted, my mum threw a towel around me but the damage had been done. I refused to wash in the sink again! My mum said we could close the curtains in future but I was adamant that I was seven and too big to still be washing in the sink. Later as I was having my bedtime cocoa Dad said that from now on I would go the public baths with him every Friday night.

I never liked the trek to the baths along Shawbridge Street. It was little more than half a mile, but Pollokshaws was starting to get run down as the area had been singled out along with the Gorbals for major housing redevelopment. Businesses had started to close and the closes boarded up as the City Corporation compulsory purchase orders went through.

It was a process that lasted three years

before the demolition and construction. What followed was dust, then mud - five years of bulldozers and pile-drivers. For four of those years I went every Friday to the public baths.

I needed it. My primary school was right in the middle of it. There was no escaping the destruction of the backyards, the library, four churches, the shops, the gardens, the streets, the homes of everyone I knew. The baths were spared - so in the midst of the incessant sound of the pile drivers ... that was relentless twenty-four hours a day for two years - I had the greatest luxury in my life.

Each bath had its own walled cubicle tiled to the roof. A bath cost sixpence. The bath was enormous. It was pre-filled by the attendant and supplied with bars of carbolic soap. You got half-an-hour of sheer soaking, honest to god hot water, and the chance for twenty minutes to forget the world.

Except for the chatter around you that echoed off the tiled walls. Dad would sometimes shout and ask if I was okay, other times the attendant would be joking with somebody, so it was public in that sense, and for a young kid it took me quite awhile to totally relax and enjoy the cleanest place in Pollokshaws.

Pollokshaws had been a wealthy little fabric and print manufacturing village from the tail end of the seventeenth century up until 1912 when it was incorporated into Glasgow. The city had brought electric street lighting and improved tram links and the village ultimately became more urban than rural. Yet for me it still retained a rural charm.

The fields were two hundred yards away - the Green Knowe led to Kenishead along a road that was as old as the first Stewarts. Cows, horses, sheep - there was a blacksmiths, and even a dairy. The Estate farm had a piggery and also bred Highland cattle.

But just to make you get this into context, right smack through all of this ran the London Midland Scottish railway line - Glasgow to London.

Yes, I was a train-spotter.

It could not be avoided. Specky Smith got me into it. He was almost three years older than me and my mum trusted him to let me go train spotting with him by train from Pollokshaws station to Glasgow Central. Its ironic when I think of the novel and film Trainspotting, and that having met Irving Welsh a few times, that train spotting was my route out of Glasgow.

I gave me my first excuse to travel. And boy did I use it. Every line in Glasgow. Every train depot in the west of Scotland. I told everyone I was train spotting - I underlined the names and numbers - but it was an excuse to get out the house - sit on a hilly knoll, hang off a Victorian bridge, play tennis-ball football in the station platform, climb an embankment, watch the signalman, wave to the passengers, write down exotic place engine names and dream of seeing more.

I loved those engine names, especially the Jubilee class - Trinidad, Tobago, Tonga, Sierra Leone, Seychelles, Mauritius, Zanzibar. It was a tour of the colonies. It had me pawing over maps - so much so that my mum gave me greaseproof paper so that I could trace and colour in the countries I had discovered from my train books.

I became quite skilled at tracing. I prided myself in my own maps. It was all only possible because my parents had been sold a set of Arthur Mee's Childrens Encyclopaedia by a door-to-salesman in 1961.

It was the best thing my parents ever bought me - my whole life would have been different without those books. I had a home reference library of my own.

From that time, if anyone gave me a fact, I could check it, accept it, dispute it; I had the power of information. Years later I coined a small phase that is still up the Palm Tree office - Information is money, collect it!

The coinage Arthur Mee gave me filled my coffers. My school marks improved incredibly. I was top in geography and history every six month exam for the next five school years. It was the train spotting that steered me - Ajax, Leander, Agamemnon - I'd look them up in the Arthur Mee.

It was a lot more contemporary than the bible that I also read. The bible was good for my morals but not much help with my schoolwork. The Jubilee class engines had names like Bechuanaland, Basutoland and Nyasaland. Train spotting challenged my ignorance.

Geography and history, eh? That sums up movie making - where and who. I always like to think of my films as being a location and story ensemble. That's what I admire about David Lean's work. He picked great stories, but he picked locations to match them.

Michael Powell thought to do this sometimes, and then he would decide he could create the location at Denham or Pinewood Studios. Alfred Hitchcock knew he had to have both story and location, and often he would ditch the story narrative just to get the location into the film. Ridley Scott likes to find locations but fill them with sets like Kubrick (and Lean sometimes).

Ken Loach, Mike Leigh and Shane Meadows are urban filmmakers who make locations look like everyday human environments. I am sure they would agree strongly that the geography of their films is every bit as important as the story.

I don't enjoy making urban location films as much as the open landscape ones. I am always ready to break free - get away from the urban dreariness. I like the fresh air, the chance to watch the journey of the sun through the day.

Shooting in cities can be more miserable than the worst conditions out on a mountain. At least on a mountain you can always come down and say the weather got the better of you, but in the city it is people and intransigence that sometimes precedes a desolate day.

ISLANDS OF THE YOUNG

When I was ten I was stranded on an uninhabited island.

It was the first time I saw a bottlenose dolphin. It came up alongside us and we got such a fright we nearly capsized the boat. Tommy Hamilton clung to the gunnel, Roddy MacKay and myself prayed, and the master's son turned white.

We thought it was a whale!

Our school teacher in the stern Mr. White was by now a wreck of a man, his idea of taking four of the boys out on a row in the bay had resulted in us being swept off into the Sound of Mull and on our way to America. Despite our rowing and our baling we were getting further and further away from Tobermory.

With the current against we tried to steer towards the last bit of land jutting from the shore before the open water. We succeeded in pushing the bow onto the rocks and I managed to jump off with Roddy and tie the painter to a small shrub clinging for life on the grassy edge.

We were not happy about the situation but we were glad to be ashore. Tommy had a mars bar, and in one of those sensible situations where you think everything is a matter of life or death, we shared it out except with the teacher who declined.

He was in a terrible state and rightly so - he had endangered our lives and we now had no respect for him at all. We organised ourselves and explored the rocky terrain. We discovered fairly quickly that this piece of land known as Calve was a small-uninhabited island just off the bigger island of Mull that we had sailed from. (Today it is a popular haunt for divers as there is a seventy-metre vertical sea cliff rich in sea life. Back in 1964 it was just a grazing place for a few sheep.)

We sat down and pondered if anyone would ever find us. We belonged to a party of eighty kids on a two-week school summer camp. We had been scheduled to spend the two weeks in Aberdeen, but a breakout of typhoid in the town from contaminated Argentinian corn beef resulted in a hasty change of plan and accommodation in folding beds in a Tobermory school.

After two and a half hours we discovered the island was separated from Mull by a sandy tidal channel that revealed itself in the falling waters. There were a few seals around - we waited another half hour then I tested the crossing by wading across. The rest followed and we were back on Mull.

We met the police car two miles along the dirt track round the bay. My second experience of the police. They were overjoyed at finding us safe and well. They were not so pleased with Mr. White.

When we got back to the school we were taken into the big kitchen, fed whatever we liked with double helpings of ice cream. Mr. White was sent packing on the last ferry back to Glasgow. We never saw him again.

We were heroes. I had always been popular, but after our Robinson Crusoe adventure, I was the most popular kid at camp.

The following day we played cricket, I was out for a duck, and I was still cheered. A girl fell in love with me and taught me how to play *Can't Buy Me Love* on the piano. As she crammed up with me on the piano stool with me, it was the happiest moment of my life.

Ten years and four months old will forever be the age at which if my life had stopped still I would have been happiest. It was my Peter Pan moment. At last everything in my life had come together - family life, school, and my personal well-being. I had overcome all my childhood illnesses and disadvantages and I had prospered into a tall, blonde, good looking kid who was good at sport, tanned easily, made friends quickly, and who had emerged as a leader amongst my own age group.

I was even liked by my teacher and that is saying something after the start I had had.

At the age of five, I was the first and only

kid to get the belt for disrupting the class. It was made clear to me that my first three primary teachers Mrs Walker*, Mrs MacIntosh* and Mrs Browning did not approve of me much.

But at ten, I got Miss Graham - she was a fair and brilliant teacher - and I was one of her favourites in a very short time. I was still quite a cocky kid and during one lesson about the skin on our bodies, Miss Graham stated at everyone had freckles. I put my hand up.
"Yes, Robert?
"I don't have any freckles, miss."
Miss Graham took up the challenge and asked me to come to the front of the class. She studied my face and pondered. Boys were still in short trousers in those days, so I rolled down my school socks to show her that I had no freckles on my legs.
She asked me to roll up my sleeves. She inspected my arms and found not one freckle, not even a blemish.
She was quite sweet about it and said to the class that I was right, I had no freckles, and it was good to remind ourselves that everything we think that is true may turn out not to be true at all.
At the end of school that day, my classmates searched all over me for freckles until they too concluded that I was completely freckleless.

Its a funny old world - freckleless, my skin olive coloured, my hair blonde, and my eyes brown in winter, green in summer, I somehow still managed to look Scottish. It has to be the B- blood.

I have a few freckles now on my hands and chest due over exposure to tropical sunlight, but I still seem able to produce enough melanin to turn most uv radiation into heat rather than burn. Maybe I should thank my mum more - she always made sure I was protected from the sun - I remember a string of dodge looking sun bonnets and hats in my early years that I absolutely hated. In winter I was not allowed to go to school without a hat and scarf.

Miss Graham only belted me once. It was for train spotting.

It was in the first term we had her as a teacher after the daunting Miss Browning and her last holiday slide show - the wonders of Egypt - the only thing of wonder in Miss Browning's class of Friday spelling B's and constant fear of punishment.

I was waiting for the 12.05 Express for London to roar through Pollokshaws West station that I could see out the window from front row left in the class. We sat in rows according to our placing in the previous half-year exam.

The 12.05 always had Britannia class engines steaming them along - they included Oliver Cromwell, Owen Glendower, Hereward the Wake and their likes and they were amongst the most spectacular shielders of their day.

I was waiting and waiting between the reading lessons for the 12.05, hoping that it would be an engine I had not spotted before. Then it happened. I could feel it coming, the excitement as it roared through the station on its way to London.

"Robert!" I was totally jolted out of my euphoria. "What are you doing? "I'm train spotting, miss".

There were a few giggles.

"Come out here." I knew what was going to happen. "But Miss, it was Britannia."

To no avail, I put my hand out and got belted.

At the end of class five minutes later, Miss Graham asked me to stay behind to have a word with her. She let me explain how important train spotting was to me and that Britannia was numbered 70000 and that it was one of the most important sightings I had ever had.

I went on to explain that Britannia was built at Crewe. She was the first British Railways standard locomotive to be built and the first of fifty-five locomotives of the Britannia class. She had her cab roof painted white. This was to commemorate her pulling the funeral train of King George VI from Norfolk to London following his death at Sandringham House.

Miss Graham got my enthusiasm and apologized for belting me but pointed out that she could not allow me to daydream in class and stare out the window waiting for trains to pass. I said I was sorry and showed her one of my train spotting books with all the Britannia engines I had seen and underlined. Geoffrey Chaucer (70002), William Shakespeare (70004), John Milton (70005), Robert Burns (70006), Alfred the Great (70009) etc.

I could never have done that with Miss Browning. From that moment I realised that a teacher could be a child's friend as well as a mentor, and with all my years of education, Miss Graham stands out as the one who understood me best, and got my best out of me. Maybe life was not a fix.

It is impossible to really remember everything about childhood. The image becomes one of the painter - the self-portrait - there is a resemblance but there are also lies - simply because we want to make ourselves appear better than we are - or more likely because we do not have the skill to portray ourselves as others see us.

Memory loss has a lot to do with it - I think I've forgotten more things than I've learned. It is also hard to say if Tommy and Archie Hamilton had more influence on me than Roddy Mackay or Alec Houston, or if I learned more about girls from Rosaland Smith and Muriel MacDonald than Josephine Crilly and May Melaney.

Whatever was going on, I was growing up, becoming the adult that would take me all over the world and into the movie business.

But back then; did I know what I wanted to do at the age of ten?

My grandfather George Moffat born in 1888 had gone to sea at the age of fifty-three. He had lied about his age and enlisted in the Merchant Navy in 1941. He was torpedoed twice on the Russian conveys, both times ending up in the water. He remained in the Merchant Marine after the Second World War and was retired at seventy-two when his real age was discovered.

He was a character. I was watching the news on TV after school one evening when grandpa popped up in a street interview on whether he drank cod liver oil or not to keep away colds. Remember this is a man who was been torpedoed twice? He took the bottle from the interviewer and drank the whole lot.

My mum was aghast. I was as proud as punch. He was a real man - he had hair on his chest, did not suffer fools, did his own thing. He encouraged me to become a marine engineer when I grew up.

My abiding memory of him is the days trip my young sister and I took with him to Edinburgh. I got to train spot, clamber over the castle cannon, and eat ice cream. I took my mum's camera so we still have some pictures of that day.

Picture taking is a common occurrence in modern times - digital photography has revolutionised the ease and immediacy of capturing images.

Certainly most families had a camera when I was young, but it was the family camera and it was used for holidays and special occasions. Every day life was not captured - when photographed; most people were in the holiday clothes or were dressed up for a wedding or social gathering. Nowadays photography captures the normal as much as the super-normal. Except in movies.

I was starting to make notes about life - small diary entries, dates.

On the 2nd July 1965 I started two notebooks. The first called Notes on Anything became my own fantasy football jotter. I had my own FA Cup won by Wolves, Scottish Cup won by Aberdeen, European Cup (Dulka Prague beat Real Madrid 2-1) and World Cup - Scotland beat North Korea 4-3 in the final and the Scottish goals were scored by Baxter (2), McCreadie and Lennox. I had a British Cup - Man City beat Aberbeen 3-2 in the final - I had a Fairs City Cup in which Hibs beat Barcelona 2-1 - a British League Cup (Celtic won that with a 3-0 drubbing of Liverpool). Scottish teams were great back then! The team entries are all in blue ink, the scores in red. It is meticulous and reveals a neat and tidiness long since gone in me.

The second jotter is more revealing. It is marked Films, The first two pages list the forty-seven Biggles books I had read up to that date. It is hard to explain about Biggles, they were the ultimate in boy adventure books. Biggles flew all over the world with Algy and Ginger and got into all sorts of scrapes.

The only boy adventure book that I ever read that beat them was *Treasure Island*. The spirit of Jim Hawkins was in Biggles, I was secretly Jim, along for the ride with Biggles over jungles and exotic dangerous places.

I had plundered the ancient local library and exhausted its shelves. At ten, now popular but precocious, I had asked the librarian if I could borrow from the adult section. She was indignant. Ten-year-old boys do not read adult literature!

I said politely that I had read all of the children's books and there was nothing more for me to do but reread them, and which I felt I did not want to do. She did not believe me, so I asked her to test me on my knowledge of the children's books.

Tintin, *Hardy Boys*, *Biggles* (of course), *Famous Five*. I could reel off the plots of every one. She looked me up and down and capitulated. I got two adult tickets to go with my four children's ones. Common sense won the day.

The jotter marked Films (like the Sun newspaper) starts proper on page three - The Films I Have Seen. The first film entries are *Military Policemen*, *The Spy With My Face* and *Goldfinger*. The list that follows is more than three and a half years long and ends on 18th March 1969 with film number 589 - *Oh! What A Whopper*. I had done my time, I had reached the age of fifteen, I was done with lists. My sister Carol, six years younger, kept the list going until the end of the jotter on 19th Oct 1974 with the entry *The Great Lover*, film number 1015.

I was watching a movie every second day. In the 60's, that was probably normal, a mixture of weekend cinema with television. There are some notable cinema films that had lasting effect on me. *Mary Poppins* (no,5) for the magic I tried to resist, *Magnificent Seven* (no.9) for its morals, *Lawrence of Arabia* (no.27) for the revenge massacre of the Turks, *Zulu* (no.385) for the warriors, *Privilege* (no.466) for its insight into class differences.

These are just a mere fraction of the thousands of films I must have watched to date, but as a child you are more influenced in your thinking and the images live with you longer.

I was a compulsive list maker, ticker, and under-liner as a child. The train spotting also became bus-spotting and plane-spotting, my traveling however local, became more extent; the film listing made me ever more ready to watch films over any other kind of entertainment; the fantasy football made me glean the sports pages for more and more team names to match with places on my home drawn maps traced from Arthur Mee.

I was driven by names - the need to have new names to put new meaning to - with each name came a new concept of how the world was built, where it worked, and how it interconnected through sport, machines, and film.

Yet although I was curious about far away places represented by football teams or in movies, I had not conceived the idea of one day going to these places, to find out for myself what was behind the names.

I sometimes wonder if I had not been so interested in names I may have had a happier life. I was looking at the stars the other night and Orion was standing out clear overhead. I remembered back to my time on the Amazon when I had a star chart and tried to memorise the names of as many of the constellations as I could.

Now in hindsight I may have made a mistake in doing this. The joy of the stars is the vastness of the universe: knowing a few random points takes away the pleasure of looking at the canvas that scientists think is thirteen billion light years in radius. What am I ever going to know about things out there?

I made a stab at trying to understand the sheer incomprehensibility of it all when I made *Dark Side Of Heaven*. I failed. So far all we have is theories. If you have the answer to why we are here and how it all started, let me know.

Back then I only knew Scotland. All of our family holidays had been in Scotland with the exception of the Isle of Man where we spent three fortnights - 1960, 1962 and 1967. Isle of Man looks pretty much like the south west of Scotland where I came from - even the names of the two biggest towns Douglas and Ramsay are Scottish names.

So it was a novelty, aged sixteen, when I first went to England with my family on a camping trip to Cornwall. That was a long trip in a Ford Cortina with mum, dad, Carol, my six-year-old brother Allen, and Stuart Aitken my best friend from secondary school. We did not want to repeat the journey back, so as sulky teenagers, we set off to hitchhike home to Glasgow.

It was my first real experience of Hippies. It was a life-changing journey ... I read a lot about the Sixties these days but no one really mentions that the ethos that started in that decade carried on until the arrival of Punk in 1976.

The mass movement of kids was more a Seventies event than a Sixties one and I certainly got caught up in it big time. 1967 was the year of Love and Peace brought to us by the Beatles and Scott MacKenzie. At school six of us were sent to the headmaster to be belted for wearing remembrance poppies behind out ears. Opposition to Vietnam became a political movement in 1968. Woodstock in 1969 put it all into words.

By 1970 the kids of the West were on the move and I was one of them. I had grown my hair into a mass of curls, went hitchhiking and youth hosteling every second weekend, and sang folk songs. I learned the lyrics to every Bob Dylan and Donovan Leitch song. I also started drinking a lot of beer but that was because I had not yet been offered any drugs. I was only sixteen. The school organised a summer field trip to The Shetlands for the upper school geography pupils. There were thirty one of us and we stayed in the Lerwick at the town school that they converted into dorms. Stuart and Gordie were on that trip along with the swots like Alex Harvey and Sheila Kay. It was the last time that I remember being what you refer to as a child. We wanted to get into mischief but we didn't have the cash or the knowledge of how to misbehave badly. Even the girls that studied geography were on the boring side. And besides, it was The Shetlands! We may have sneaked out for a few pints but in general it was cups of coffee in the local cafe and watching the seagulls trying to steal fish from the boats.

The most memorable part of the trip was a visit to Sumburgh Head to look at the Beaker settlement in the shoreline. That really was something special - 3500BC stone houses built into the dunes. Since then I've seen something similar in South Uist, but it was not exciting as seeing its kind for the first time. I had the chance to return to Sumburgh eight years later but it was by helicopter. A helly-port had been built right next to the stone houses, and as I changed from one helicopter to another, I briefly glanced towards the place where I had spent one of the last days of my childhood.

Drugs came to me a year later in the form of a lump of hashish. I had left school and got a job as a gardener cum pot scrubber at the Invercauld Arms Hotel, Braemar. I was a good pot scrubber but my gardening was woeful. I had been cutting grass and trimming hedges in Glasgow since I was fifteen to make some pocket money. It was my first business - I bought a pair of garden shears and went door-to-door selling my services. However, that was not the same as looking after the garden of a hotel the Queen visited every year for the Highland Games. When I planted some border white heather along the front of the hotel garden, it all died. I was saved by the arrival of my exam results that confirmed that I did not have to go back to school and do sixth year. I had passed all my subjects and was on my way to university. I left the hotel trade.

I had been accepted by Glasgow and Strathclyde universities and wrote to each saying that I had accepted the offer of the other. Clever, but also stupid. I wanted a gap year (it wasn't known as that then, it was a cop out). I wanted to go traveling in Europe.

In reflection what I did was do the Grand Tour before going to university. I learned to view it as this fifteen years later during my second stint at uni. Like Wordsworth, Coleridge, Byron, Shelley and a thousand romantic imitators, I went to view the classical world. I did not know that was what I was doing but that's how it turned out.

However, not being a noble son or of rich parentage, I took the savings from my weed pulling and dish washing and hitch-hiked on an overcast day in July 1971 with a cardboard sign that said 'South'. At 2am on a foggy M1, I was dropped off near London by some Freaks traveling in a red van. One of them pushed a lump of brown stuff into my hand and told me not to smoke it all in one joint.

I did not have a clue. I was wearing an ex-German army parka and put the lump of brown stuff wrapped in silver foil in the small zipped pocket on the left sleeve just below the German flag sown so brazenly on the khaki coat. Remember, this is just twenty-six years after Hitler had fried in the bunker. All was still not right in the world and memories were long. But I was making an effort to help the world get over it – it was up to our generation to rebuild the new world that our parents had fought for.

Unfortunately there had been a few scares along the way – communism, the Cuban missile crisis, and the Indo-China conflict, now fully developed as the Vietnam War. You have to have lived at that time to understand the futility of the Vietnam conflict. The opposition to it was global. The moment Johnston sent in the bombers to destroy Hanoi, that was it, the moral argument had been lost. Although there are strong parallels with the Iraq conflict, the scale of Vietnam was altogether something else. Two and a half million US men served in South East Asia. To get five hundred thousand men on the ground, the Americans had to draft its youth into the ranks of the army. They did not want to go. They were my age or a little older and they called themselves Freaks – men who had been trained to kill but who wanted to be Hippies.

In 1971, when I got across the channel to Europe, I met them in droves, and I continued to meet them for the next four years until on May 1st 1975, when Saigon was abandoned to the victorious Viet Cong. At the moment the news came through, I was in the Swat Valley in Pakistan with a Vietnam veteran who was one year older than me. He cried. It was over. The Vets, the draft dodgers, the anti-war exiles could all go home to America. It was a humiliating time for a nation that had won the Second World War (with our help of course).

As a kid who had been fighting all of his life, I had no desire exert my will or bully or kill on behalf of Britain. The Vietnam conflict had made me a pacifist, but only in relation to Vietnam. I did not know that at the time. I was against all war but perhaps there was an underlying fear that the US (and allies) and the Russians had enough nuclear warheads between them to destroy the planet. We had been brought up with the newsreels and the hypothetical nuclear winter scenarios that would follow. We were all scared of the consequences, so it was common sense as much as ideology that made me a pacifist in my early adult years.

Look, at the end of my life, assuming I've got plenty more years, I might look back and say – as a young man I was naïve, as a middle aged man I was ill-informed, and as an old man, I am just a fool. I have my opinions – some of you may agree with them, some of you not. None of us are the full shilling - we have our hobbyhorses and our dancing bears – we ride them or we make them dance to our own tunes.

But certainly I know that Vietnam formed the global policy of my generation – live and let live - the resultant free trade mantra that gave rise to global capitalism until the crash of 2008. Dominance by capitalism is economic colonialism but surely it is better than military colonialism if you are a pacifist by nature. The breakdown of capitalism and the void it leaves is a free for all – that is the opposite of free trade and it creates a dangerous vacuum of shortages and anarchy – theft and bullying returns.

I saw it as a kid – you are forced to stand and fight for what you believe in – free speech, free trade, free association. You hate it, but you are forced to do it. Britain and the Second World War. That's as good as an example as we are ever going to get. Turn back the pages of history – it repeats itself – but please, not in my lifetime – lets try and keep the peace.

My first continental experience was Ostend. I met up with my school friends Stuart and Kenny. We went for a beer. It was all lager and when they handed over the small schooner I complained. 'What's this! Its half froth!' Oh the ignorance of youth! I have been educated in the ways of foreigners now, I accept frothy beer and skinny chips.

My first night on foreign soil was in a sleeping bag on the beach under an upturned boat. It wasn't the most memorable beach night of my life, but it was the first of hundreds of beach nights around the world. I must have liked it.

I do not really want to go into detail about

that first journey to Europe that took me to Brussels, Luxembourg, Trier, Nuremberg, Munich, Innsbruck, Venice, Lake Como, Lucerne, Geneva, Verdun, Paris and home. I wrote a poem about it called the *First Journey of The Wanderer* and it sort of covers the geography of the experience. What it doesn't really spell out is what it did to me.

Up until then I had been an adventurous, but studious boy. After the trip, I just became adventurous. After seventeen years of institutionalisation (if you include my nursery years starting at four months), I had gotten a glimpse into the bigger world beyond Scotland.

When I got back to Scotland at the end of August, I was clear that I did not want to go to university in Scotland. I don't know why, all my friends were going to university in Scotland. I wanted to be different; I was even accused by one of my friends of being deliberately different. I did not see it like that – I just wanted to experience life elsewhere. At seventeen, outside of Scotland, only Oxford and Cambridge took in undergraduates younger than eighteen.

Well, they certainly were not going to let the illegitimate son of a cleaner into their ranks, so I had to wait a year to get a place at Newcastle University. In the meanwhile, I had to get a job. I considered taking three months training at British Army boot camp as the pay was really good, but I had a dilemma. I wanted to be a hippy. I was well suited to discipline, as I had progressed through the Boys Brigade to colour sergeant before I quit the year before. However, I was worried that if I signed up, I might like the army and stay on. It was a possibility.

Meanwhile I went back to Braemar for the Highland Games and to see my old hotel work mates. One of them, Don, showed me what to do with the lump of hash - smoke it. My first toke of hash was perched on the side of the Mar river below the village bridge hiding behind a small tree while the Queen opened the Games. I was not used to tobacco never mind hash. It was a baking hot day and I had to lie down to stop from throwing up. It was good practice for later when I was in Afghanistan and couldn't get up for three days.

Back in Glasgow, I had a second job offer: to train with the Bank of Scotland as a junior clerk. I hummed and hawed. The bank informed me that because of my school qualifications I would get an extra fifty pence a week for every Higher that I had. This mounted up to an extra two pounds fifty a week. On a base rate of nine pounds fifty a week, I would be getting twelve pounds a week. The army were offering close to eighteen.

I took the bank job. It certainly was not a glamorous job, but they sent me on day release every Tuesday to Langside College to learn accountancy, economics and Scots Law. To this day I am grateful to the Bank of Scotland – not for shackling me to clerk serfdom in the Ibrox branch, but for having the foresight to train their staff in the rudiments of banking. From the college lessons during my time at the bank, I learned the basic principles of accountancy, economics and law that have allowed me to flourish in the arts business. Without that training, I would not have made so many films.

However, like the army training, I was worried that I would excel at it, so I decided that come exam time, I would flunk the lot. I had never failed an exam before, so I had to put me some constraints upon myself. I made up my mind to not answer a single question on each of the three papers and walk out.

Sounds easy. Not so. Each one and a half hour exam had a compulsory half hour sitting before being allowed to leave. Do you know how agonising that is when you have been trained to excel all your school life and a paper lies in front of you and you know most of the answers? It is difficult to do nothing. But my will prevailed – I answered nothing and left each exam after half an hour.

I was free. I would never be able to stay on now! I had been informed that Newcastle University had accepted me on their Applied Geology course starting in late September.

I asked to see the bank manager to tell him I was leaving.

Mr. Macmillan looked just like Ted Heath, the then Prime Minister, and like Heath, he had a part share in a racing yacht. He also came to work in a blue sports car with a soft top. He was a snappy dresser and he treated the chief clerk like a minion. Fortunately, he liked me, but I was dreading telling him that I had to leave the bank to attend university.

The moment the words were out, he was overjoyed that I was not going to spend my whole life being a miserable bank slave. He went up ten fold in my estimation. He could not wait for his retirement day – banking was no place for a young man of spirit and adventure. I was better off out of it!

I left the bank feeling suitably bolstered that I had made the right decision and that life was more important than career when you are young. Just as well – when the exam results came back it was recommended that I never be allowed to sit the exams again. I had done too good a job!

I was on to my next adventure. On May 11th 1972 I set off on a proper Grand Tour. At the time I thought I was off to see Glasgow Rangers play Bayern Munich in the final of the European Cup Winners Cup in Barcelona. I got as far as Paris, met some Freaks, got put totally off track, and ended up at the *Second British Rock Festival* near Germersheim, Mannheim, out of my head on acid watching Pink Floyd perform *Dark Side of the Moon*.

I never went to a football match again (unless I was playing myself). If you've ever seen the film *Buffalo Soldiers* you will know what I am talking about. The US Marines were the drug dealers at the festival - they had everything including free PX rations that we lived on for three days. It was a happening, man! Those Vietnam veterans were flying the hashish in from Afghanistan, the opium from Laos, the acid from California. All aboard US military cargo planes straight into Wiesbaden. They had had their *Apocalypse Now* in the Vietnam jungle and they were now making sure that they never went back up the river.

Those guys were tough cookies. I was eighteen and these guys could not have been any older than twenty-four, maybe twenty-five. They were all NCO's – sergeants, corporals, guys who had cut themselves apart from the general conscripts. They were selling the drugs, but they also gave a lot of the shit away for free. They were just happy to connect, although they did look a bit out of place in their faded fatigues, boots, and dog tags sitting crossed-legged in their military tent.

It cost two pounds eighty pence (eight dollars, twenty-two marks) to see thirty five bands that included A. R. & Machines,

Abacus, Amon Düül 2, Atomic Rooster, Beggars Opera, Buddy Miles Express, Curved Air, Ekseption, Eloy, Family, Frumpy, Rory Gallagher, Guru Guru, Home, Humble Pie, Incredible String Band, Karthago, Kinks, Linda Lewis, Lindisfarne, Albert Mangelsdorff, Max Merrit, Milkwood, Osibisa, PacificGas & Electric, Tom Paxton, Pink Floyd, Quiver, Sam Apple Pie, Spencer Davis Group, Status Quo, Strawbs, Uriah Heep, Wind, Wishbone Ash.

Good luck getting that these days. Lets just recap here – The Kinks, Status Quo, Pink Floyd – are legends in their own right. And the rest! A list of British rock in 1972 minus the Rolling Stones. Hendrix was dead, the Beatles broken up, Led Zepplin burnt out. Everyone else on the one bill, right? Those days have gone. And all for less than ten pence a band. Where has the world gone wrong?

Do I remember much of it – very little? As they say about the Sixties – if you remember it you weren't there. Same in the early Seventies. But I did remember everything about Pink Floyd. I was on acid – say no more. I was one of seventy thousand kids to experience that weekend. Afterwards, I thought that nothing could ever beat it, and I never went to another festival although I have been tempted to go to Glastonbury more than once.

The rest of my four-month second European trip was something else. It included sex, drugs and on and off Mediterranean ferries. I hitched down through Yugoslavia to Greece and went to live on the beach Mykonos. I didn't plan it; it just turned out that way. The US Sixth Fleet took their rest and recreation on Mykonos – there was always some ship docking off shore and sailors on twenty-four hour leave coming ashore in lighters with everything you would ever need for a party except girls. They were kids my age worried about the nuclear warheads they had on board their ships and what they would do if they were ordered to fire them.

To the casual visitor, Greece seemed to be booming in 1972, but an atmosphere of pastoral life remained with food, accommodation and transport being cheap. There was no inflation, with the drachma pegged at 80 drachmas to the pound. Indeed, ouzo cost less than 2 drs, and a plate of egg and chips 7 drs.

Greece then was under the dictatorship of George Papadopoulos and his junta. It was difficult to ignore the white shirted, black trouser, moustached men of the Aliens' Bureau, whose members would turn up now and then to check our passports. It was not me I was worried about – if we got into conversation with a Greek about anything, these same men would question him. They were not always gentle. Greece was not what it seemed. Most memorably the junta treated the Greek people in the same manner as Greeks treated their dogs – they were kicked viciously, and starved. It was a cruel time.

I was just an eighteen-year-old kid – but I had eyes in the back of my head. The authorities were heavy on drugs and nudity, and gods help you if you were caught doing both. It was straight to jail. It was regressive regime and there was an undercurrent of tension in all aspects of daily life. Politics seemed to be the only topic of conversation, though openly talking about politics was taboo.

So we lived on the beach, took our drugs in secret, and never took all our clothes off unless it was the beach on the far side of the island where you could see the cops coming. It was too long a walk for them from the town in the midday heat along the three-mile dirt track to Paradise Beach, so they came by motor launch.

We were always quickly dressed and drinking something in the one bamboo taverna that stood on the beach in those days by the time they waded ashore. The cops always tried to pick some 'chick' out with binoculars on the way in, but once we had our clothes on, we all looked the same. Occasionally some uncool dude would argue with the cops. They'd shake him down for all the money he had on him then take him away just the same, and put him on the next ferry off the island.

It was a game. The cops were just as tired of the raids as we were. They were just seen to be doing their jobs. We were just a bunch of foreign kids, hanging out because Mykonos was a cool place. We were not the type of tourist they wanted to attract, but we were about the only tourists during the junta years. None of us could have been older than twenty-one or twenty-two. A few had been to Turkey and Israel, but the real far out cool dudes had been to India and back.

India. That was the place to go. It was the dream of nearly every young kid I met that summer. But you needed money – it was four thousand miles overland from Greece to India. I counted my paltry savings and decided that I had enough to get to the two thousand miles to Morocco at the other end of the Med.

What a hastily drawn up plan it turned out to be. I had been on the beach about two weeks with a guy called Henry from Lake Tahoe. We had befriended a Scottish girl who had taken a shine to me, but Henry wouldn't leave the two of us alone together, he clung to me like a chaperon.

It was Henry's idea to go to Morocco. He wanted that girl. I was indifferent, so he ended up hitching with her in Italy after we crossed the Adriatic to Brindisi. It was a big mistake giving up the girl – I couldn't get a ride. It took me three days to get down the sole of Italy and across to Palermo in Sicily. I was a wreck.

Not so Henry and the girl. They were as fresh as daisies. Apart from having to fend off an amorous truck driver who had wanted the girl as payment for the ride, they had slept in a barn, a hotel and had a third night in an undisclosed locale. I was as mad as hell with them.

We got on the ferry for Tunis. It was a pleasant enough sail across the Med to Africa – on board I met Henrik from Berlin who rolled up a big fat joint. Henry abstained.

When we got to Tunis, they would not let us off the ship. "Why not?" I asked. A single word came back from the Tunisian immigration officer "Hippies!" They took our passports and they were not handed back to us until the ship had set sail back to Italy.

So there were the five hippies – Henry, the Scottish girl Lynn, Henrik, a German girl, and me, still cruising on the Med, the sun going down, the moon coming up, it was lovely. Except that it was not. We were not heading back to Palermo, we were sailing for Cagliari in Sardinia, another island.

We were called into the purser's office and made to pay for the trip. It was pay or be arrested in Sardinia. Not much choice then? By the time I had paid I was left with about enough money to get back home. Henry and the girl got off too. That Henry - he was a smooth operator. He also had money.

Henrik and I hitched northwards and spent the night on the west coast of Sardinia in a haystack. I remember it as being quite beautiful and have always wanted to revisit that quiet sleepy coastline with its old run down farmhouses. That night had the most enormous moon I had ever seen, the crickets were singing – the heat of the day radiated from every stone you touched. It was magical. It was one of those golden moments when the worst is behind you and life can only get better. We shared a bottle of wine, some bread and cheese, lay in our dry warm haystack, and I felt truly contented and blessed. For despite the difficult week I had encountered, it was behind me, and I had come to no harm.

The following day we overlooked the straight that separates Sardinia from Corsica. Ahead were the white limestone cliffs of Bonifacio and the tumble down town perched precariously above. The birthplace of Napoleon. France. And there standing with us was Henry and the girl. They did not seem to be getting on as well as before, and I was glad.

They had decided to take the ferry from Calvi to Marseilles and travel down into Spain and across to Morocco from Algeciras. I did not have the cash for that and I wished them luck. It was a genuine parting, no recriminations, we were kids, we did not know what we were doing, and life was one big experiment. We would live the real thing later.

Funny one that? We all plan to follow the monkey path until the monkeys take to the trees. More on that later.

Corsica turned out to be quite a bustling island after the slow life of Sardinia. We hitched a ride easily up to Bastia where we could catch a cheap ferry back to Livorno and the Italian mainland. However, there was a snag. The next ferry was not for six days.

What do you do in Bastia, Corsica for six days? You eat bread, cheese, yoghurt and drink the cheapest wine you can find to starve the boredom. I've been a lot of places, but Bastia was not one of the best of them. It was an ugly town, perhaps it still is. It is also the only place where I have had all my possessions stolen.

With no option but to wait the six days out by sleeping on the beach, I slept every night with my backpack under my head. On the fifth morning, I woke to find my face in the sand. My pack had been stolen from under my head! Passport, vaccination papers, diary, clothes, soap bag, camera, boots, everything!

Corsicans! Oh la la! I got out my sleeping bag, searched around the beach, then found a trail of my belongings scattered in the sand and up the steps leading to the promenade. I found my passport, vaccination papers, diary, clothes, and almost everything else except my boots, camera, cooking stove, soap bag, my German parka, and my backpack itself. I reported the theft to the police in my schoolboy French, listed the stolen goods, signed a piece of paper, and that was that. Except it was not.

Four months later I got a letter from the Bastia police that stated that they had caught the culprit and that he had been sentenced to nine months in jail. Still, at the time that was not much comfort. Fortunately I had slept with my jeans on and the last of my money was in my back pocket. But I had to buy a cheap old French army canvas rucksack, a cheap pair of sandals, and a toothbrush. It was not that cheap.

By the time I got off the ferry and put my feet on Italian soil again, I had twenty pounds left. Henrik had decided to hitch back to Germany and asked me if I wished to come. I thanked him but I told him I had decided to go back to Greece. He didn't think I was crazy, but I certainly knew I was.

It was a rash decision but I have never regretted it. From the moment I left Livorno and up to the point I finally spend my last penny, I worried about what I would do when I ran out of money. When that moment came I started to think about how

I could make money.

That's a curious thing about life – we strive to make our way in the world, and when we do, we worry about losing the world we have made for ourselves. Likewise with money – we fear losing it more than we do about earning it. We have no fear about earning money; we only have fear about it not earning enough to sustain the world that we have built for ourselves.

So take me – the young eighteen year old kid in Italy with twenty pounds in his pocket? Here were my choices. One. Return home to Scotland after being away for six weeks and get a job. Two. Go back to Greece with nothing, live on Paradise beach, and work out how to make a living.

What made me do it? Don't know. Pride? Stupidity? Stubbornness? Two quid was less than one day's wages. I had to be crazy, right?

We all have turning points in our lives – this was one for me. I've had many more since, but at the time, it was the most consciously willful decision that I had made since I knew I had to beat cousin Hughie in my first fight. Remember how that turned out? I won and got to ride the bike.

This time round, I took the beating. It was the end of June, the sun beat down on me on those open roads, no hat, no screen protection, nowhere to get into the shade.

My face got so badly burnt; my nose became a single blister. It took many years for the burn scars on my nose to disappear. That was bad enough, but when I got stuck on the road outside Zagreb (now Croatia) and had to spend the night in a ditch, I got so badly bitten by mosquitoes, by morning my eyelids were that swollen I could hardly open my eyes. It was agony.

To add to my ignominy, in the dark I had slept in a ditch in a field of burnt grass and was black with ash. It was one of the worst moments of my life. Yet what could I do – I got back on the road and stuck out my thumb.

You can imagine the looks I drew when I got into cars, but despite being in a foreign land, most people were kind and generous, I was fed and watered, and allowed to continue on my way with kind words. The only hostile time I had was in Nis (now in Serbia) when I was sleeping in a doorway and was hustled out of town by a night policeman who would not let me rest.

What I did for money I do not know. I was picked up by a hippy couple who took me into Greece. What a contrast to six weeks earlier when I had been clean clothed, bright faced, all kitted out with my tent, and with the luxury of traveling by train from Belgrade to Thessolonika and staying in the youth hostel.

Something had happened to me – I had

become a tramp. I wasn't a hustler, it was not in my nature, but I was learning to get by on my wits. I was not following the monkey path.

DROP OUT

I never set out to be a dropout. I got caught up in the times. After my summer in Greece I was restless and just could not get my head down to study. As I took up my course at Newcastle University, I was thinking of only two things – drinking beer and having sex with as many girls as possible.

Both of these things happened simultaneously. I arrived in Newcastle on September 28th for Fresher's Week and went crazy. Six days of excess and getting to meet as many other students as possible. The Friday Night Fresher's Ball band was The Kinks. Yes, The Kinks. There was no formal wear or any ball gowns. It was three hundred teenagers crammed into a space in the Union. Ray and his brother were arguing on stage. They were drinking bottles of whiskey and vodka. I know this as I stole their bottle of vodka while Dave was arguing with Ray. Is there a better song than *Lola* to sing along too? *Waterloo Sunset, Sunny Afternoon, You Really Got Me, Dedicated Follower of Fashion, 20th Century Man*.

Yep, we were twentieth century dudes. Drunken ones, stoned ones. I forgot to mention the availability of hashish. It was cool to be a dope smoker at that time. It was the preserve of the young. Nowadays, pensioners, once hippies, toke on weed and *charis*. It is no longer cool, it is a way of life for many. Its something I have grown out of, but when I was young, it was a means of communicating with others my age. What I mean is, we learned to share, smoke a pipe of peace, so to speak. Perhaps that is a crazy analogue, but at the time, I really think that sharing a joint with someone or in a group was part of the understanding that we were all in it together. But in what together? Well, it was condemnation of the Vietnam war, apartheid in South Africa, the British army occupation of Ulster. On the flip side, we were for equal rights, the end to all forms of discrimination based on sex and colour. We were peace and love, man, except that most of my fellow students did not have a clue, and did not care. Many of the female undergraduates did not believe that women were down-trodden. They were doing all right, so why couldn't every other woman be doing what they were doing. I met quite a few of these Roedean kinds of girls. They just didn't get it - probably still don't. The battle of the sexes they called it. Men have always been dominant, you can't change human nature, it's the way things are, I'm not a feminist, they are all lesbians and I don't want to meet any.

How things have changed - but because of the peace and love movement, not in spite of it. People say that the revolution happened in the 60's. Yes, it did, but it was the change of attitudes in the 70's that made Margaret Thatcher possible. Heaven forbid that I helped Maggie to become

Prime Minister (I left the country for the USA three days before the 1979 election), but I am glad that I have always treated women as my equals; my life has been richer for it.

For my first two university terms, I was accommodated in the Castle Leazes Halls of Residence. The halls lay up the hill behind the university that led to Spital Tongues. The halls had been built on the town moor and the icy North Sea wind that swept eastwards across the north Tyne valley made my hair a knotted mess. I was used to wind as a Shaws boy, but not the bitter East Coast blasts that made life miserable. That is what I have always hated about Edinburgh. The architecture is a medieval wonder, but the cruel breeze that blows ten months of year off the Forth is the reason why most Glaswegians detest the place and run back to the warmer wet of the west coast.

The halls themselves were composed of three houses that faced on to a quadrangle with a carp pond. I was in Eustace Percy Halls, and as a grant aided student, I had opted for the complete package that included getting my meals provided in the halls' canteen. I signed up to play for the house football team and played centre back as I had for my school team. The strip was awful - we looked liked clones of Aston Villa, West Ham and Arsenal. I'm not sure which we were supposed to be, but it was not an inspiring set of colours to play in. Eustace Percy wasn't a great name either.

Invariably we lost, and it was summed up by our right back who also played for the University team that we were a bunch of wasters who preferred to drink beer than win. We sort of agreed with him and vowed to try harder, but we never did. The half-time orange was always followed by the full-time skin-full of beer which at that time was ten pence a pint in a pub, but maybe six or seven pence a pint in the student's union. Fifty pence bought a lot of beer!

From playing football, I met my drinking buddies Kim Hunter from Matlock, and Geoff from Kidderminster. We each had a tiny room barely big enough for a bed, a small desk and a chair, but for the first time in my life, I had my own room. While this seemed odd to many of my new student friends, most of whom had come from more affluent, and mainly southern backgrounds, the novelty of having my own space went to my head. For much of my first term I was out of control with my drinking, my daily routine, my everything that I had ever known.

I was also in culture shock. The liberalism of English life was a complete bewilderment to me. I was at sea with the conventions and norms of English customs. I didn't know its boundaries and I just assumed that there weren't any. In reverse, I was a curiosity to many of the English students – I appeared to be wild, adventurous, open, and above all, honest. Too honest sometimes. I soon discovered my forthrightness was sometimes interpreted as being rude.

Finally, after years of exploration, near misses, and absolute frustrations, I lost my virginity to Maggie in my small single-bed room. She was all of one year older than me and took control by getting on top of me. She was a lovely girl, but I was, as I said, out of control and off seeking other sexual adventures with Christine, Sue, in fact, anyone who showed interest in me. It was 1972, and women were being liberated by themselves through the teachings of Germaine Greer, Valerie Solinas etc. The sexual revolution was full on – and I read these weirdly fascinating feminist books to understand how I could be a better man. In *Scum Manifesto, (Society for Cutting Up Men)* Solinas appeared to be a right man-hater because of her lesbianism - she had some valid points, though the shooting of Andy Warhol appeared extreme to me at the time. Now that I understand that she thought Warhol was stealing her work, I can cut her some slack, no pun intended.

However, Germaine Greer was a whole different kettle of tea - *The Female Eunuch* - she made complete sense to me. Women had to take control of their own destiny, but men also had to understand how they unknowing were suppressing woman by upholding conventions fashioned by men - religion, secular laws, the family unit. In my view she was the architect of *women's liberation* in the UK, and her book reaffirmed my own upbringing - that women did not need to be the equal of men- they just needed to be themselves. Her insight into the neglect and shame with which women viewed their own bodies was particularly poignant. The 70's youth movement is sometimes classified as the Me Generation, but it was not about the mind, it was about the body. The Me referred to being free and open about your looks, your bodily functions, not to be embarrassed, but to enjoy bodies as beautiful things that should not be closeted in buttoned-up shirts or bras. (In contrast, the 00's Me Generation was about acquiring material wealth, and we are all the poorer for it.)

Some of the girls I met at University had read *The Female Eunuch*. If they hadn't, I suggested they should. It was more revolutionary than reading Plato's *Republic*, Darwin's *Origin of the Species*, or Einstein's *Theory of Relativity*. We were at university for god's sake. You were supposed to read books. I was having sex with these girls and none of us really knew what we were doing, but Germaine Greer certainly pointed us in the right direction. As a man I had a duty of care towards my partner. Lovemaking was about just that - not sex. I took me some time to work out what love was. From time to time I was asked if I had heard of Germaine Greer. Word was getting around.

My first day of lectures was October 3rd. I

went to Durham with a girl called Judy to visit some of her college friends. Why I did that I do not recall, I have a vague memory of being in the quad near the cathedral, visiting the cathedral and being wowed by it because it had been used as a temporary prison for three thousand Scots soldiers by Cromwell's Roundheads after the battle of Dunbar. Kept without food, water or heat, seventeen hundred of them had died. Unsurprisingly the survivors smashed the place up and burnt the wooden interior to keep warm. The destruction prompted the removal of the survivors who were shipped to labour camps in North America. The broken statues said two things to me about England - that the English are capable of severe brutality, and that the English are stupid enough to imagine that their enemies will respect their traditions if they treat them barbarically.

I recommend a visit to Durham Cathedral, I have periodically visited it since that time. It always imparts the same reminders to me - and I hope that visitors are smart enough to understand why the Scots smashed up one of the finest examples of Norman architecture that is now a World Heritage site.

Missing my first day of lectures set the pattern for my university life - girls were more important than study, beer was more important that getting a degree. I found the course work boring. No-one had forced me to take up engineering geology, but I was starting to wonder why no-one had suggested that I did not need to study for a science related degree. It was just expected that if you were Glaswegian that you would be an engineer of some kind - mechanical like Watt, physical like Kelvin, electrical like John Logie Baird. There is no concept of the artistic Glaswegian - art was the preserve of Edinburgh with their Robert Louis Stevenson's, Arthur Conan Doyle's, and more recently JK Rowland (though she is not Scottish). Whether it was writing, art or architecture - in Glasgow the bright kids were trained to be marine engineers or civil engineers. Some got to be doctors, but again, Edinburgh had led the world in medicine for a hundred and fifty years, so it really was no contest.

Nope, my destiny was to be an engineer, or an explorer. Yes, I had forgotten about that side of Glaswegian nature. We like to get as far away from Glasgow as possible. That repulsion (rather than reversion - I do love my native city, I just can't live there) is the driving force that we cloak with pretence that we are seeking knowledge about the world. Information is money you might call it. If we are armed with the right information, then the money will follow and we will get rich! People are always remarking to me how friendly the folk in Glasgow are. I agree with them, but then I point out why. They are curious about you, as they want to learn everything you know so that they can profit from it. It might cost them the shirt off their back, but knowledge is to a Glaswegian the greatest source of wealth. They want knowledge for the sake of possessing wisdom, owning something that others don't have. In other places neighbours compare their wealth by their house size or model of car - in Glasgow it is about whether you know that Glasgow means 'green place' or 'blue place' depending on whether it is a Goidal name (Irish) or Brythonic (Welsh).

Just for the record I think it is the latter. I am Protestant and bias towards blue, but Glasgow was in the kingdom of Strathclyde (that later included Cumbria and the Isle of Man) from the late fifth century to the twelve century and was a Brythonic speaking land just like Wales. I grew up with these Brythonic names - my speech is that of the soft-spoken south Clyde Glaswegian, not the rasping nasal Glaswegian who comes from north of the river. I can hear the difference - it's as plain as York from Lancaster, only subtler.

I was having a hard time getting people to listen to me at university. I could understand everything they said to me, but many could not understand me. I put it down to one thing - they were not listening. Those who took the time to listen caught almost all that I said except for some of the unique words and phases we have in Glasgow like 'the ba's up in the slates'. That aside, what I discovered was an intolerance of the vernacular, the richness of the language in exchange for a formalised, almost rigid vocabulary that bordered on the boring.

One of the reasons I liked Kim and Geoff so much was that they had colourful turns of phase, particularly Kim. His Derbyshire accent was thicker than my own. He was all 'Eh, op and all tha' and I loved it. I understood everything he said. Same with Geoff with his south Brummy drawl that pronounced Kidderminster as 'Kiddy Monster'. It always made me laugh.

Yet, these boys were very smart - we were part of the mere ten percent of kids that managed to get into university in those days. It was extra difficult to get into a good 'red brick' uni unless you had demonstrated that you had the aptitude to study. Oxford and Cambridge? You are kidding me, right? Actor Chris Bearne who is twelve years older than me and has played such wonderful parts for me as Hemlock Crab *Crab Island*, Jackie Shields *Villains*, and Roger Harris *Third Falcon*, told me that going to Oxford on a scholarship from his humble background in Exeter was 'to be sent up to be put down'.

In Newcastle, I had that same experience. I was ridiculed in every way imaginable about my accent, my nationality, my upbringing, my step-father's profession, my schooling, my manners, my behaviour, and above all, my intelligence. I was lumped in with those Scottish prisoners-of-war in Durham Cathedral. I was a heathen with a course tongue, dubious heritage, and poor prospects of making something of myself.

I soaked up very insult you can imagine, kept my temper, and ultimately learned about my taunters' weaknesses - conceit, ignorance, intolerance, and the inability to empathise with those who were not clones of them. These are the sorts of guys who now pass anti-immigration laws to preserve an English way of life they have invented. Kim and Geoff on the other hand represented the real England to me, and I loved them for it.

I talk here only of the boys. The girls liked me because I had none of the traits that I have listed above. To them I was refreshing. It was my mission to get them to read Germaine Greer so they would change society and eliminate the next generation of male clones they ultimate would produce! Yes, sometimes my uncontrollable wildness was unattractive, and I admit that I was very bad at committing to pre-arrangements - dates etc, but in general I was very popular with girls from all backgrounds.

I had no understanding of wealth. My first sight of real wealth was Mr. Quine's abode in Kent a few months before, I have written about Mr.Q in my poem *The Wanderer Part 2*, so I had no preconceived notions of anyone's parental upbringing. However, I was a very good listener and I was repeatedly troubled by their tales of how their lives were controlled by their parents through money that was drip fed if they did what they were told. I felt compassion for them - okay my upbringing may have been one of relative poverty, but I was loved - what I was hearing was that a private education from the age of seven, a gap year, then on to university, was a tale of neglect and emotionally deprivation.

Time and time again I was hearing the same thing - these teenagers resented their parents for giving them everything they thought was good for their future, while the kids were crying that their parents did not love them.

Something, somewhere, was wrong with the whole private school educational model and more likely still is - it was a system designed to create clones who in former times would be offered or given jobs in the colonies. They would not have a problem ordering servants around due to their inability to empathise; the rest of their duties could be ably carried out with conceit, ignorance and intolerance. Such virtues carried many colonials a long way in the tropics if you read the history books.

This was Newcastle in 1972 and many of these girls were struggling with their upbringing. They did not want to be Stepford wives, and with the exception of Karen Hancock two summers later who was bonking me on the side except when her boyfriend or parents visited, I doubt any of the girls I got to know would have been stupid enough to take up with one of the boy clones. Who knows? Money sometimes wins, and understandably. I don't remember Germaine speaking on why so many conditioned privately educated girls put security before love. If today there is more Jean Brodie's teaching in private education than I suspect, then it will be a triumph for women.

By early December university, and Newcastle pissed me off. I went to Edinburgh for the weekend to see some of my old school mates - Stuart and Gordie Ferrie who were studying there. They had gone home to Glasgow for the weekend and I hung out with John Hunter, Gordie's red-headed flat mate, and went to two parties with him. I realised that Edinburgh was much more formal than Newcastle and that life was slower. Stu and Geordie showed up on the Sunday and I spent the last of my cash in the Chambers Street Union bar. Returning to Newcastle in a better frame of mind, I was determined to get my head down and take my studies more seriously.

What was I learning? Some of it was tedious - the maths, physics, chemistry - the basics. The dry part was the geology. The interesting part was the mining and civil engineering. We got to learn about mines, pulleys, lanterns, gas, and everything you can imagine about coal mining. There were six students on my course in total, fifteen in the entire department. It was one of three universities in the country to specialise in engineering geology. Once I had a degree I was guaranteed big bucks in Zaire, Zambia or Zimbabwe (Northern Rhodesia back then). I was on to a gold mine (sic), but the thought of spending two years working down a copper mine in Zambia was depressing.

Two of my fellow students had been seconded from the British Coal Board. They were both young miners who had worked their way up into management. They were family men with kids and both were Geordies. The clones had a field day with that kind of student, but I liked them for their down to earth ways and their droll humour. They always seemed to have to go home, so apart from the odd lunchtime pint, I didn't get to spend any out of class time with them.

Another fellow student was Brendan. Within three years of graduating, he had made a small fortune with a Middle East company who paid him to sit on their board to give their operation credibility. He didn't have to attend the board meetings, and I know this as fact, as my South American travelling buddy Charlie ran into him in a bar in Panama City in 1978, and he was living off the his 'consultancy' money. Charlie came back to Taboga Island out in the Gulf of Panama and told me that Brendan was thinking about becoming a writer, and I thought good on him, he's come round to my way of thinking. I regretted not seeing him myself.

On my course, I had the highest academic qualifications, but I was the youngest, and totally inexperienced in the ways of the world. The mining lads could pass a mining exam without opening a book, and two of the other lads had some sort of industrial experience. I was already getting the idea that the course had to be whittled down to four students in year two, and that somebody was expected to drop out, and another to switch to straight geology. The weakest student on paper was a lad a year old than me called Dave who lacked personality as well as a top-drawer brain. The red lights were flashing all over him that he was the weak link. The problem was that though I was academically strong and stood no chance of being the weakest link, my heart was not in it, and it showed.

On December 15th, the last day of term, I had a geology exam in the afternoon, but instead of going, I remained in the pub at lunchtime and had eight pints. By three o'clock I was pickled and sat in the Union foyer talking merrily away to a girl from Oxford called Kate Piggott who was going home for Christmas. We were sitting right under the big Union tree and passing the time until she caught her train to Oxford, and I caught mine to Edinburgh. I was quite taken by her. She was petite, even featured, and bright and she loved her parents. She had not read any Germaine

Greer. We got on like old friends and I was charming and witty, though in reality I must have been completely drunk.

When I got to Edinburgh, still pretty pissed, I went to Goschen House to find Stuart. Jindy (Rajindar) one of my classmates all through secondary school answered the door and let me in. Jindy Singh Bhopal came to Scotland from India with his family when he was five and had been the only non-white kid in our class at Shawlands Academy. Stuart had the same last name as me - Aitken - and in class we were arranged alphabetically as Aitken, Aitken and Bhopal. We were in the top class, so we were also the first in the register at role call. That lumped us all together from day one. Anyway, Jindy studying to be a doctor, was not a great drinker, after a couple of pints he was always sick. Today he is listed in Debretts as Professor Raj Bhopal CBE, and has chaired the World Health Congress on Epidemiology. On his lists of interests is hill-walking and travel, and myself and Stuart must take responsibility for getting him out of the Strathbungo house shared with his larger than average family.

When Jindy was twelve he was one very shy boy. He was not in the least sporty, but we were in the school chess team together with Stuart. It was Stuart who got him into cycling. He was so good at chess that he cycled to the European Junior Chess Championship in Groningen in 1972. He finished sixth! I played chess with him forty nine times before I beat him, and then I refused to play him again. I was like that back then. The other forty eight times, Jindy taught me some of his best moves and I should have thanked him more for what he gave me.

Anyway, we stumbled down to the Golf Hotel near the Meadows where we found Gordie and Kenny MacIver causing uproar. I didn't help to quieten things down, and after ordering a pint, we were all thrown out by the landlord. Drunk as we were, Gordie started to scramble over parked cars like a kangaroo, then fell off. By this time, Jindy wanted nothing more to do with us and disappeared. We decided to make our way to the Chambers Street Student Union and on the way, we were stopped by two policemen as were kicking traffic cones all over the road. Let off, we had another four pints in the Union and after that everything went a bit hazy.

Following day we started all over again after watching Scotland lose 13-12 to the All Blacks at Murrayfield. Doctor Stuart, now a Psychologist and Visual Impairment Specialist at Edinburgh University, joined us and thereafter we certainly tried to see how badly we could impair ourselves. Jindy skipped the action, so the four of us headed for the Student Union. Due to the UK becoming a full member of the European Community in 1972, by the end of the year all men's bars had to admit women. It is difficult to find any reference to that now, but it was a major shift. Some pubs openly defied the new order, but resistance in general fell away as most men welcomed the change with the exception of places like the Royal and Ancient Club in Saint Andrews. It opened the door for pubs to become more open planned - the snug bars reserved for men or women were taken out. Germaine I think approved.

On December 16th, Teviot Row House, the preserve of the drunken male Edinburgh student had its last night as a men's bar. Gordy, who has been an exemplary deputy head at Lockerbie Academy for many years, bought the first bucket of beer. Yes, they were only serving the beer in ten pint plastic buckets at £1 a bucket. After our bucket was empty, we just dipped into everyone else's.

The Armstrong rugby squad, the top team at Newcastle University was there. I knew one of them, Steve Buckner, and together we organised the singing from our vantage point on top of a table. When everyone else started to climb on the tables, mayhem ensued. Not to be outdone, two of the All Black team, after doing the *Hakka*, got on the bar and did a strip tease. When they finished, they could not find their clothes.

The last thing I remember is the Chinese lanterns that covered the overhead lights in the bar being set on fire and the bar being evacuated. We left the Union with a bucket of beer just as the fire brigade arrived.

What an evening.

Life as student was everything it was supposed to be but I really was not happy. I took a vacation job as a relief postman delivering Christmas mail from Pollok roundabout, along Brock Road by the old Bellamine Academy site (where I lost my chess match to the girl), and back to where the shopping centre was later built, which has now also been demolished. It required little mental application but involved a hell of a lot of walking, and one dog that really scared the shit out of me.

It is true what they say about postmen - dogs just don't like them. I put it down to postmen wearing red clothing. If a dog were a bull, it would charge, right? If a bull were a dog it would bite, right? Warped logic but feasible. The worst thing about being a Postie was the early start - clocking at eighty o'clock on a dark frosty morning is a student's worst fear - that he is destined to be another clone. The upside was the pay - I earned £15.63p for five days work. In spending power that worked out at one hundred and fifty six pints of beer in a regular pub, and almost two hundred pints in the Student Union. I was loaded! Worker wages had a lot more punch to them in the 70's.

After Christmas Kim, Geoff and Paul, another friend from university, arrived at my parents flat the day before Hogmanay. My eight year old brother Allen had to give up his bunk to Kim and share with my twelve year old sister Carol, while Geoff and Paul got to sleep on the floor. It was a crowed house - my parents place was a kitchen and living room downstairs, three bedrooms and a bathroom upstairs. The bedrooms were not large, but they were cozy and we had moved into 32 Shawholm Crescent when I was eleven.

Like so many things from my childhood, these four-storey flats have now been demolished. It just seems crazy that after Pollokshaws was demolished and rebuilt in the 60's, that in the 00's, it was decided by Glasgow City Council that it had be demolished again and rebuilt. I now wonder what the original landscape of Pollokshaws ever looked like. When houses have no perceived value, they are flattened. The idea that an area the size of The Shaws could be demolished twice in forty years is inconceivable in London. Four thousand people in constant displacement. Too many engineers and not enough artists with some far reaching vision? I think so.

My life was not all about alcohol as a student though Kenny, who was studying at Glasgow University, and I did do a pub crawl of ten pubs in Shawlands with Kim and Co. We actually managed nine - Corona, Bay Horse, Georgic, Marlborough, Sammie Dows, Doune Castle, Shawlands Hotel, Rogano, Quaich but missed getting to the Newlands Hotel by last orders. These were my teenage drinking haunts during my rights of passage. Unfortunately, we forgot that Kim and Geoff were Jack the Lads as well, and that despite our happy state, they found themselves in the verge of a fight with two middle-aged hard-nuts who still fancied themselves as young bucks, (the stupid twats). We whisked them out of there. Hard to believe that Kim after graduating went on to work for Halliburton and Chevron in oil exploration. As I write this he is now Doctor Hunter and a vice president at Hewlett Packard in Sacramento.

Following day I took my university friends to Loch Lomond to show them the beautiful side of Scotland. We had a quite day with a pint in the Duck Bay Marina, another in the Colquhoun Arms at Luss (now gone), and a ramble back to Balloch. The loch has featured in a number of my works. I shot a few scenes of *Love The One You're With* around Balloch, Sarah Maguire's swimming segment of *Got To Run* at Luss, and her climb of Ben Lomond. I describe the entire length of the east shore of Loch Lomond in my poem *Along The West Highland Way*. I shot the scenes of the frozen waterfall and loch scenes in *Lost In The Landscape* around Inversnaid.

Loch Lomond remains one of the most beautiful places in the world for me. From my early experiences going day-tripping there with my family, youth hostelling at Rowardenan or Inverbeg or Loch Lomond Castle, camping at Luss for my eighteenth birthday, making love there on the beach in my thirties and writing poetry, filming there in my forties, returning there in my fifties to film some more, Loch Lomond has remained a magic place.

There is nowhere quite like it and I have been to many places. Lake Toba. Lake Titicaca. Lake Navasha. Lake Nicaragua. Mangerton Lake. Lake Como. Lake Atitlan. It's up there with them as a contender as the most beautiful lake in world. Geoff thought so, he could't stop telling me how beautiful it was. But after all, he was from Kiddy Monster.

When we got back to Glasgow in time for tea, Hogmanay was just one big piss up with my old school friends and my new university ones. They eventually went home, and apart from a visit to Edinburgh for the day, life settled down until I returned to Newcastle and the grindstone.

That's how I felt - burdened doing something my heart was not in. I reconciled with Maggie and had a night to remember. Two days later I had a note from Kate Piggott that she would like to go out with me. The following evening she was in my room having coffee and we were moving towards being intimate when Maggie walked in. I said the wrong thing. Maggie got upset with me, Kate got upset with me.

Three days later I was in the middle of explaining my relationship with Maggie to Kate when Stuart, Gordie, Kenny, John,

Jindy, Doris White (our local MP'S daughter) and Hazel (Stuart's sister) showed up. I failed to talk Kate round and that was the end of what might have been a beautiful relationship. Totally dejected, I took comfort in the bed of Saucepan Sue who was also in halls.

Sue appeared to be quite open to having sex with any one of us, but Kim was fussy about his women, and Geoff had a girlfriend back in Kiddy Monster. Plucking up the courage after being rejected by Kate, I took a saucepan and knocked on Sue's door to ask her if I could borrow some milk. She read between the lines and invited me in, and after listening to my sob story, we got naked.

It was my second time with her and she was not the shy type. She perhaps was too easy, but maybe it was the other way around. It was a mutual no-strings attached exchange that ultimately was just two young people having sex. It was nothing very sophisticated, but being young, we had lots of energy. Whether Valerie would have had me cut up, or Germaine would have disapproved of Sue's easy virtue, I don't know.

My ego was bruised by my own stupid actions and I needed some reassurance that I wasn't a failure in the sexual revolution. I don't remember that Sue and I ever really talked about anything - she was not a great conversationalist - and I probably wasn't that forthcoming despite what I think I had said to her.

What my school friends did that night I don't recall except that I think Hazel ended up with Kim and Doris with Geoff. We never discussed the intimate details of our relations with girls with each other. In that sense we were shy, embarrassed and respectful of the girls we were sleeping with. As for the Scots boys, surely they did not all sleep in my room? Anything seems possible considering the quantities of beer we consumed when we got together.

Look, I'm not going to lie to you. Re-reading the letters that my friends sent me - Stuart, Kenny, Hazel, Gordie, Bill we were all neglecting our studies and really struggling to get our heads-down. Gordie had twenty-two pints on his birthday and Kenny felt bad that he only had seventeen. On top of that I was getting letters from Glenn Martin, a Canadian I had hung out with for six weeks on the beaches of Mykonos the previous summer. He was in Israel going from kibbutz to kibbutz living on zero cents a day. He couldn't get laid as the Israeli girls looked down on him and all the foreign students were back in college. He had a lot of pointed things to say about Israel and the way in which life was organised there. It put me off the country for life. In one letter he told me had just spent a week down a copper mine in Eilat getting paid a dollar an hour. Fifteen of them were given, goggles, picks and shovels and made to work a twelve-hour day. After a week he was fired and a new bunch of 'volunteers' hired. He wrote me that e was all for helping the Arabs take the country from the Israelis.

I was also getting letters from Sue Forester who I had meet while youth hostelling in Cockermouth the year before. She was a few years older than me and we had struck up a pen pal relationship. She was a bull breeder at that time and her handling of bull's testicles made me ... well. Let's say that I was not mature enough to handle the thought. While at Eustice Percy she wrote to tell me that she had left Cornwall and had taken up a job at the Kingussie Centre that seemed to be some sort of teacher training place. She was hired as the cook but that she really wanted a job with the Post Office. She suggested in every letter that we should re-meet sometime but we never did. Life is like that.

My mother wrote to me regularly and always gave me a run-down on life in Glasgow. She would write to tell me that there were few Corporation buses on the roads as the mechanics were on strike; or that there was no bread because the workers were on strike; and less beer for the same reason. In the same breath she would inform me that she was sending on my moldy hiking boots and that my pencils were inside my shorts that were inside my boots. She also reminded me that the three pounds I borrowed was to pay my university fees. She didn't mention what she thought I had spent the money on.

My cousin Robina, my terrible twin one-day younger first cousin, always got a mention. Not sure if she approved of Robina being out with her work mates at the Doune Castle in Shawlands, and staying over. She was not imprudent enough to say that Beanie was drunk. I only ever saw my mother sip an alcoholic drink once at a family New Year gathering - it was sherry and made her giddy and unwell.

My mother also kept me up to date on the achievements of my bother and sister. Allen won second prize at the Boy's Brigade party at Halloween - he was dressed as a Rajah's page for the second time. The costume must have set something in Allen's mind because he went to India some eleven years later when he was nineteen. As for my sister Carol, I got the news that she had broken her right wrist jumping on a trampoline and she was getting better at writing with her left hand.

My Grandad was still alive and my mother always had an exasperated tone when speaking about him, probably because he had abandoned my Granny in 1941 for a life at sea when my mother was thirteen. She was the youngest of the five Moffat children; there had been a sixth - Robert - who had died at the age of seven. I was named in memory of him. My mother was nine when that happened and it left a deep lasting affect on her, so much so that I believe it is why she cared so much about children. She was a second mother for many of my cousins and their youngsters. Her advice was always about having enough warm clothes or a hanky at hand because of the frost in the morning and the frozen puddles.

The best letter writer was Stuart's sister Hazel Aitken. She was ten months older than Stuart and that made her about a year and a half older than me. She was studying to be a teacher at Hamilton College and like the rest of us; her life was about parties and getting bevied. I don't know where we learned this hedonistic way of life - none of us came from well off families - all of our parents had gone through the Second World War, rationing, and doing without things.

Hazel wrote to tell me that she had a bust-up with her parents about her lifestyle and that she wasn't going back home until her birthday. Hamilton was only eight miles from Glasgow, but in those times, no young folk had a telephone or a car. If you wanted to call someone you had to use a red call box or one of those gray pay phones that hung from a wall and looked like something from Gerry Anderson's *Thunderbirds*. (Many year's later I met Gerry and Sylvia at Pinewood. I much preferred Sylvia.) It was much easier to write a letter - even second class got there the next day.

In Hazel's communications with me she would be chirpy and always mention music - spacing out to Santana (and turning it up so I can hear it), and missing lectures and hearing that they had played Pentangle and things. It was Hazel who had made me put my ear right up to the speaker of her parent's old one piece mahogany gramophone and listen to the whole of Marc Bolan's *Ride A White Swan* single six times. She really turned me on to listening to music at volume, rather than just sitting gently nodding and tapping my foot.

Not that I was ever likely to have turned out that way, all of us were listening to Jimi Hendrix and Cream when we were fifteen. Not forgetting *Sergeant Pepper's* when we were barely thirteen. We were brought up on British Mod and Rock music and Bill and Kenny bought the NME so that we missed nothing, or anybody we hadn't heard of. Hazel and Doris, her best friend who had been the school captain in the year above Stuart and I, liked folk music and the pretty boys like Bolan, and we were being trained by them to like the solo artists. It wasn't until *Straw Dogs* that I so got it that Davie Bowie became one of my favourite artists of that time. There was no one to touch Bowie for coolness - not even John Lennon or Mick Jagger.

Hazel, however old fashioned she may have seemed to others, did more than just drink - she went to see *Lady Sings The Blues* or *Clockwork Orange*, though she didn't know what to think of Kubrick. I went to see it in the Haymarket Cinema and was blown away by it. In later years I don't know what all this talk is about the picture being banned - Hazel saw it in Hamilton, and I saw it in Newcastle. I would call that a fairly general release. Somebody has been rewriting the history books.

Perhaps it was the cultural side of Hazel that Kim liked in her - they had a thing going for a little while - and like many youthful relationships it just fizzled out. The last time I saw Hazel was at Stuart's wedding in 1975. I was supposed to be the best man, she the bridesmaid, but as life can sometimes go topsy-turvy, Gordie was the best man, and some other girl the chief bridesmaid. Hazel and I sat at the back of the church together miserable at the turn of events. To have your sister and your best friend pushed to the back told us something about Stuart we had not noticed before. After the reception, when I hugged Hazel and went back to Newcastle, I saw neither of them again.

Back in Newcastle I took up with Maggie once more after an evening at a student disco. I had called on her room just before the Christmas break but she had left a note for me saying that she had gone home and would see me the following term. It had hurt, but I had hurt her with my failure to spend time with her rather than my drinking buddies. We reconciled and had a night in bed to remember.

The following day I missed a geology field course. To make matters worse, I missed the following day's course as well. I was fined fifty pence by the department headed by Professor Stanley Westoll. Yes, fifty pence - I'm not sure what kind of punishment that was except it was the equivalent of six pints of beer in the Union bar. Ten days later I feel asleep in a lecture and I was told to leave the room. It was embarrassing as it was in front of my fellow students, but it did not reform me. The last day of term I went across the road to the Poly with Nigel Denton, Sam and Mick to meet with a girl and drunkenly blew most of what I had left of my grant.

My relationship with Maggie is the one that I should have paid most attention to, but I was stupid. She really liked me and had been my first true lover. As she was a year older than me, she was more experienced in life and was clearer about what she wanted from it. I didn't know what it was that prevented me from committing to her; it was something to do with my upbringing that prevented me from knowing what love was.

She had fallen in love with me but I just wasn't listening. I wasn't chasing after her or wanting to spend any time alone with her. I was always with my mates living it up, cracking jokes, and being happy. But deep down I wasn't, I was hiding my unhappiness by never being alone. In fact I no longer enjoyed my own company, something that I certainly did enjoy on my two trips around Europe before I got to uni.

In hindsight I was in culture shock. This struck me many years later when I moved to Somerset and suffered some of the same anxieties and uncertainties that I experienced in my first year in Newcastle. I was a stranger in a foreign land, but I was an immigrant, not just passing through as a traveler. It seems inconceivable now that a Scot could see England as a foreign land in the same way that a Pole or an Estonian might. But it was certainly the case that I was at sea and at a loss in working out how I should behave and what was expected of me now that I was living in England.

When I tell people this story now they laugh. Newcastle is not England! Well, Newcastle is more England than London. The first English (Angles) settled in Northumberland and gave their name and their language to what we call the English. They defended English life and culture from their ancient enemy the Scots for well on a thousand years, and in the process clearly defined the border between the two nations. In contrast I was from Glasgow, and brought up in a fiercely proud Scottish family that was purely Scottish in roots, with its protestant work ethic, that had seamen and miners as breadwinners, and women with home-making skills that allowed their male children to become engineers and explorers.

We were a family who exported skilled people, to other parts of the world, but not to England. We did not consider life in England to be beneficial to Scots, for history had taught us that Scots who went to England, became culturally English in order to fit in.

This partly has become my fate and is as natural as a chameleon that changes colour with its background. But of all the countries that Scotland does not want to lose its people to, it is the Old Enemy, as it swells its numbers. Of all my Scottish school friends, I am the only one who went to study in England. As far as I know, I am the only one who presently lives in England, so to them I probably have been lost.

And lost I began to feel as I approached my nineteenth birthday. I had lost the place with my studies, and I had lost my own cultural certainty because I realised I had to change but did not know how. I thought I was coping but I really was not.

Its painful to think back on that now as a write this section of my story at the age of sixty. My life is completely different - today for example the summer heat wave given to us this year requires every window and door in the bungalow I live in to be flung open. Outside on the cricket field, I can hear the village team bowling at the visitors with great whoops of delight when they have a success.

My life in Buckinghamshire is one of privilege and tranquility even though the parish council is trying to evict me from the bungalow after more than seven years of tenancy (that is another story). Later this afternoon I am off to Shaw's Corner to watch Chris Bearne play Mazzini Dunn in *Heartbreak House* on the lawn of Shaw House. Chris is delighted that he does not have to play Shotover and has confessed at seventy-two that he doesn't feel old enough to play the part anyway.

At eighteen, I was not old enough to play the part of a responsible student. Kim and I hitchhiked to Edinburgh for a party with a crate off Newcastle Brown ale. You can imagine the surprise of the drivers who picked us up, but once they knew we were students (what else could we be with our long hair, hipster strides and parkas), we weren't questioned about the bottles rattling in the crate. At the party I got locked in a bedroom with a girl called Margaret, but I don't remember a thing about her, where she was from, or what she looked like.

Unfortunately, at the end of the second term, being a geology student, my term was not over. The following day, I had a seven-day field trip in Skye to take part in and the eleven-hour coach trip was excruciating. I was down to my last fiver and the next day was my nineteenth birthday that I spent on a wet miserable

Sunday in Broadford.

We were staying in the Broadford Hotel and Stuart hitched up from Glasgow. Kenny took the train to Kyle of Lochalsh - and as the son of British Rail worker, he had a one third-price rail card that the used regularly, much to all of our chagrin. They pitched a tent in the hotel garden.

They felt right at home in Skye as we had youth hosteled there together several times. In fact, I was the only Scot in the entire forty-person party, so it was nice to have my pals there to explain Scottish customs to the students we were getting drunk with. We had a quieter time than we had had at Luss the year before, but I still got bevied. Professor Battey, sitting with his newspaper and sipping malt, smiled smugly upon my friends and me.

Two days later, after a wet day in the field with our geology hammers smashing at rocks, Dave (The Weakest Link) and I had the idea to play a trick on the other students. In a drunken haze we decided to put sand in everyone's bed. This single action changed the course of my life by ending my academic days. We made the error of not putting sand in our own beds, so it didn't take long for Battey to point the finger at me. We even made it easy for him by bursting in on him in his pajamas in his bed – we thought he was downstairs sipping his malt – but no, there I was standing with a wet bag of sand in my hands telling him that I had gone into the wrong room by mistake.

Retribution followed the next morning when Dave and I were hustled down to the water's edge by the rest of the students, and swung by our arms and legs into the sea. I thought it was fair justice and that was the end of it. It wasn't.

Battey called me to his room and proceeded to lecture me that all Scots were barbarians and ruffians, and that I proved the rule. In normal circumstances, being lectured by a lecturer would be acceptable, but in this case it verged on racism. There I was standing in front of this Englishman who despised me, standing there in my own country being told that we were all barbarians. I was the only Scot on the course, and it was our rocks we were bashing up, it was our countryside that we were digging in, it was my country's whiskey he was drinking every night. Yet despite all that, his contempt for Scotland and Scots was that of a racist. I had found the true nature and mindset of the public-boy educated Professor Battey, and I didn't like it, or him, or what he represented. I now had his number, and those like him, and I bit my lip.

We went back to Glasgow for the Easter break, and started to prepare for exams. Well, sort of. I tried to do some studying at the Mitchell Library but I was only kidding myself that I was working. I had to wait a couple weeks for my dole and when it came it was four pounds, forty-three pence. It was hardly enough to keep me from drying up. Forty-three pints worth. I was averaging that a week at Newcastle.

On Good Friday I made my way back to Newcastle via Edinburgh. I planned to stay the night with Gordie at Gorchen House. When I turned up, I was greeted by Gordie's friend, Moira, and we went for a drink in the Bruntsfield Arms. We had an enjoyable evening and I as we were about to get it on back at the flat, Gordie showed up, and I spent the night on the floor.

When I got back to Newcastle on Saturday evening I had ten pence until I could draw down my grant cheque on Tuesday. Kim and I had left halls and had planned to get a flat together with Nigel, but they didn't show up. I was bailed out by Hemmy at 23 Rothbury Terrace who let me sleep in Sam's room for a few nights. It was a miserable Easter.

Tuesday came and we found a place to share in Heaton at 88 Simonside Terrace, an upstairs flat. We tossed a coin and I got the big front room. We were to pay two pounds, sixty-seven pence a week each. Those were the days. The place was scruffy, but we had a room and bed each, a back living room and kitchen. The toilet was down a flight of stairs in the back yard. It was a traditional North-East terrace brick row flat with outside bog.

We were on our own, no university rooms or canteen, we had to fend and cook for ourselves. It was a learning curve with the can opener, the belling hob, and some badly burnt pans. We were finally grown up and free of all constraints and interference. We were so free that one night we made a curry from dog food. It was a howling disaster.

I sat my exams at the end of May – civil engineering, engineering geology, mining, geology and maths. I got absolutely blotto'd in the Chillingham Arms the night before the maths exam and I came out knowing it had been a disaster. When the Men's Bar in the Student Union opened at six, I was there until it closed. Exams were over.

The following day I hitched south with Geoff from Kidderminster and got a ride in the back of lorry with four other kids and the lead singer of the band *Fat Grapple*. But it just wasn't our day and we spent the night in our sleeping bags on the grass at Leicester Fosse M1 service station.

We eventually got into London at 7am, and I remember wandering around aimlessly for hours and getting pissed off with Geoff for being stuck in London all day. I split and took a tube ride out to the start of the M4, got a couple of lifts, including one from a tank commander, and at Swindon, branched off and headed down to Exeter. I tried to spend the night under a mechanical digger to keep off the dew, but in the end slept beside it.

Mid morning I was in sunny Newquay, dropped off by a Tiverton surfer called Mick. I wandered around looking for somewhere to dump my backpack and eventually hid it in some tall grass above the overhanging cliff. I went for a pint, chatted up a girl from Glasgow called Margaret, then met Mick at the Western, and together chatted up Margaret and her friend again and went dancing, but Margaret was really messed up in the head. Mick and I spent the night on the beach.

A few days later, we got a job lifting twenty tons of rails and two wagon loads of sleepers. The railway line had been closed in the 60's. It was a hellava hot day and we started at eight. I had only worked half an hour when my head started to spin, and my hands blister and bleed. The other guys were struggling too. At noon, Mick and I quit. Our last act - two of us being on each end of a length of rail – was a defiant "Fuck this for a lark!" We got paid a measly two pounds fifty pence each for a body destroying four hours. The upside was that a pint only cost twelve pence back then.

Mick filled his car with me and two other guys that had quit and we finished up getting pissed in Plymouth. We ended the night in a tattoo parlour. The other two guys went first, then as the biggest guy

Mick was being tattooed, he burst into tears. That was enough for me; I got out of there without a scratch and have never been inside a tattoo shop since.

The next couple of days I sat on the beach and watched Tiverton Mick surf. Its hard to pretend to be cool when you sit on the beach and try to do board talk to girls when you haven't a clue how difficult it is to stand upright on a long slither of fiberglass. The board waxing was endless, and after awhile, watching guys fall off boards, scrape their skin off, empty their heads of all their common sense, I concluded that surfing was a mugs game.

In the years since I haven't changed my mind much – surfers are not great conversationalists, and I think that's because of what surfing does to them. What does it do to them? I don't know but it gives them a far away look as if their wits have left them.

I was back in Newcastle by the 10th June after an eighteen-hour hitch from Exeter. The only joy of that journey was to be stranded on a slip road with two lovely Brum college girls for an hour.

My last exam Chemistry was on the 12th at 9.30am. By chance I met Chrissie Brown at the bus stop outside my flat at 9.15am. She had an exam to take too. We caught the bus and had a good old natter, got off, lingered to look at the carp in the Civic

Centre pond, and still made it into our exams on time. It was a great fifteen minutes. She invited me for tea the following evening. She was a good-looking Cheshire girl and since we'd met at the Fresher's Ball when we had kissed and made out, I'd had a crush on her.

So I went for tea. In those days, tea was dinner, dinner lunch. I don't remember what we ate, but the conversation with Chrissie and her super-smart flat mate Annie who was an English student was non-stop. Everyone I knew in engineering was in awe of English language and literature girls. They were just unattainable. We were just dullards who may have read *Treasure Island* or *Moby Dick*, but we had never heard of John Donne or knew the difference between Milton and Mills and Boon. Fortunately Chrissie was a Geography student or I'm sure I would not have been invited to tea.

As it was, I loved those girls. They were bright, funny and intelligent. They were full of common sense and practical advice. I, in contrast, was drinking myself into oblivion though I didn't know it. After tea I went with Chrissie, Annie and a few of their lovely female friends to the Cochrane Lounge at the Union. These girls were more modest in their drinking habits and they slowed me down a little bit with their interesting conversation. We then trouped upstairs to a Sociology Department party where Chrissie and I got amorous on wine.

There was one unhappy moment caused by my quick tongue and rough views, but things worked out in the end and we walked back at two in the morning to my flat in Simonside Terrace where she stayed the night.

Although I had the biggest room, the bedsprings of the double bed were shot to pieces. To stop them from sagging I had wedged sideways a wooden door (yes, a wooden door) between the mattress and the metal bed frame. Part of the door stuck out and acted as a table. This was fine as long as you didn't get up to any antics in the bed. I discovered with Chrissie we were literally banging every time we did something energetic. Fortunately my flat mates Kim and Nigel had gone home for a few days.

I really liked Chrissie and she liked me, but there was sadness between us as we knew our lives were not going in the same direction. I was just too wild and she just didn't think that I was the kind of boy who would be happy to be with one girl. She had made that assessment after the Fresher's Ball. I tried to convince her otherwise but she was smart and tactful enough to make me feel wanted and not rejected, yet kept her distance so as not to fall in love with me. As if to cement this, the following night when Kim returned, we went with Chrissie and Annie to see *The Decameron* at the Haymarket Cinema.

Oh my god, talk about candid, even the cinema walls turned blue. It really opened my teenage eyes to the sexual variations and dimensions of form and figure. Those girls were wild.

But I was already wandering. I hitched a single ride from Newcastle to Hamilton for Hazel's twenty-first party at Hamilton College. The day before the party I got there about six on a beautiful evening and I sat with Hazel under a spreading tree next to the racecourse. With the sun filtering through the branches, we talked of our friends and thoughts. We were talking out the last of our innocence. We didn't want to be innocent anymore, but we were not totally happy about losing what was left of it.

Hazel was a thoughtful girl, someone that I thought had no real plan for life, but who took charge of events and situations. I don't know if she kept a diary, I imagine so, she was a vice-captain at school, you had to be organised to wear the school colours at Shawlands Academy. I know she was a romantic girl who just loved Marc Bolan and David Bowie. I never asked her if she'd had sex with my flat mate Kim. The way he behaved, I assumed it but certainly I didn't try to imagine them at it. I never saw Hazel that way, she was my best friend's older sister and that's how I related to her.

Kim joined me that night in Glasgow and the following day with Stuart we drank a bottle of wine on the train back to Hamilton. We proved to be useless at helping the girls at the Union for the party, so we went to the pub with Gordie, Jindy, Kenny etc. In all we were a party of twelve blokes, pissed, dining out on Chinese, then staggering back to Hazel's party to get further rat-arsed.

I had to cut my night short and hitchhike back to Newcastle for the start of a two-day geology field trip to Whitley Bay that I resented having to do. I was too pissed and I spent the night in a sleeping bag under an M74 flyover.

I made the field trip and waited for my exam results to come out. On the 20th I went down to the notice board at the Quad archway. Nothing. I went again on the 21st. Nothing. What was the matter with the Geology Department? The English students had had their results the week before. I woke up on the 22nd and I could wait no longer. I hitched back to the West Country and spent another night in my sleeping bag near Exeter. The following day I had taken up with Tiverton Mick again and I had a quiet week staying in the caravan of surfing dude Tony and his friends Steve, Roy, Stuart and Keith.

Pleasantly chilled out, I hitched the four hundred miles back north, stopping off on the A5 to sleep in a barn. When I got to Newcastle I went straight to the Quad arch. I'd been given a fail. I did not feel happy about it. I had failed one exam out of six – my maths. Battey called me into his office, and yes I had failed my maths by one percent. Not so bad then, except that because I'd failed one exam, I had to take them all again in September. Why, I asked. He smiled and said that it was only fair that when I re-sat into my maths exam I was under the same conditions I had been in May.

I was baffled. I thought the object was to prove that I had learned something, not see how much information I could hold and regurgitate. Not so. I was being punished for being a drunkard and a lout. He was determined I would fail, or at least, be transferred out of his department.

My summer was in ruins. On top of that, I had to go immediately on another field trip – ten days of geology mapping In Cumbria. We were put up in Featherstone Castle, a drafty cavernous place that I enjoyed for the first couple of days until the tutors starting niggling at me about re-sits. The nearest pub was three miles away – it was all a plot to keep me miserable.

I returned to Newcastle on the 15th July. My resits were schedule for the 3rd to 7th September. I had six weeks to study. I stayed with some older students at 23 Rothbury Terrace and signed on for the summer, as every student did in those days. I couldn't study staying with Charlie, Mick, Bob, Hemmy and Steve. Steve and his girlfriend Mavis were the only ones who I could communicate with. I sat at the dinner table with these twenty-one year olds and had nothing in common with them. They were all southerners. Everything they cooked was red peppers, garlic and half a bottle of wine sauce. It was inedible.

I went home to Glasgow for five weeks and struggled to study. I got laid every Saturday – Ann, Bonny, Moira. Moira, a seventeen-year-old girl with her own flat on Kilmarnock Road, started to fall in love with me. I was restless and I tried hard not to run away from my feelings. The sex with that girl was really good – she was not shy, but eventually the re-sits came, and I went back to Newcastle and 23 Rothbury Terrace on the 1st September with the belief that I had done enough work to have a reasonable chance of passing.

Three hour exams – Monday to Friday - Civils, Geology, Mining, Geology E, and Maths in that order. On Friday evening, to forget it all, I went with Chrissie to see Pascolini's candid sex-romp *Canterbury Tales* but it wasn't nearly as entertaining as *The Decameron*. My Chemistry exam was a week later.

Then the wait. Two weeks, then back to the Quad arch to discover my fate. I failed one again – the Chemistry. Jesus! So though in theory I had passed four exams twice, and two once, I had still failed. On the 21st September 1973, Westoll and Battey summoned me and told me that I could continue on at university but that I would have to change course. I told them that it was Engineering Geology or the dole. Westoll said he would give me two days to consider my options.

When I came out the Mining Department building, I turned right through the quad arch towards the Union Building. I stopped. The sun was shining and for the first time in a long time I felt happy. I jumped up on to the two-foot high brick perimeter wall and shouted "I'm Free!"

Yes, a few students turned in my direction but I just remember the euphoria I felt. The future was searingly clear as I balanced on the wall "Now I can travel. Escape. Enjoy myself!" It was a eureka moment. It was fitting that it was the day of the autumn equinox. I was going to go around the world!

Nineteen years old, eh? Where do these eureka moments come from, how often do they happen, do they happen to everyone? I honestly don't know. In my case it was my second eureka moment, the first being the need of a two year old to win his fight with his cousin Hughie or his life was going to be shit.

Printed in Great Britain
by Amazon